## EDITORIAL COLLECTIVE:

Lara Messersmith-Glavin
Paul Messersmith-Glavin
Maia Ramnath
Carla Bergman
Sara Rahnoma-Galindo
Kristian Williams

## COPYEDITORS / EDITORIAL ASSISTANCE:

Chris Dixon
Sam Smith
Em Winokur

## COVER DESIGN AND ART CURATION

Josh MacPhee

## LAYOUT & DESIGN

Lantz Arroyo

## PRINTING:

Eberhardt Press, Portland, OR

- - - - - - - - - - - - - -

For twenty years the Institute for Anarchist Studes (IAS) has awarded writing grants. This issue of *Perspectives* contains two essays by people who were awarded grants in the past, Theresa Warburton and Hillary Lazar, and three that were awarded grants to support the writing of essays that appear in this issue: Laura Hall, Alexander McClelland and Zoë Dodd. Please donate to the IAS to make it possible for us to continue to support radical writers by going to our website:
**anarchiststudies.org**

# PERSPECTIVES
## ON ANARCHIST THEORY
### N.29 2016

- - - - - - - - - - - - - - -

# TABLE OF CONTENTS

# BOOK REVIEWS

# PERSPECTIVES

# CONTACT US

The Institute for Anarchist Studies
PO Box 90454
Portland, OR 97290
perspectivesonanarchisttheory@gmail.com

Online: AnarchistStudies.org
Twitter: twitter.com/IASPerspectives
Facebook: facebook.com/
PerspectivesonAnarchistTheory

Thank you to: Aiden and Godspeed You! Black Emperor,
Charles Overbeck, Lantz Arroyo, Captured by Porches
Brewing Company, and everyone who contributed to our
fundraising campaign for this issue!

# INTRODUCTION

## THE *PERSPECTIVES* EDITORIAL COLLECTIVE

OK, editorial collective. Let's talk this through. So, what are anarcha-feminisms and why do they need their own *Perspectives* issue?

Well, because these questions persist: what's the relationship between anarchism and feminism? What critiques do feminists have of anarchists, and vice versa? Are anarchist spaces also feminist spaces, and if not, why not? Isn't feminism supposed to be implicit within the meaning of anarchism, and therefore unnecessary to specify?

Supposed to be, yes. Maybe. Depends. Anarchist organizing and socializing environments are NOT always feminist (eyeroll if you agree—we thought so). The need to confront one another on the persistent failure of practices to live up to proclaimed ideals, suggesting that anarchist cultures haven't always been able to sufficiently break free of the patterns of the society they're trying to oppose and replace, is in itself enough of a reason for stating it explicitly.

But it may be even more than that. A certain ideal of anarchism may be feminist, and a certain ideal of feminism may be anarchist, but not all the polymorphous forms of anarchism or feminism fit that description, even at the level of principles and ideals. Just as there can be feminisms whose aim might be, for example, to insert women into state and corporate power

« Art by Meredith Stern | justseeds.org

structures, or traditional religious leadership, there can be anarchisms which promote individualist machismo in the name of autonomy, or which essentialize gender binaries in the name of "nature."

Making feminism explicit in anarchism is a choice of emphasis and interpretation, among other possible emphases and interpretations. It's an argument that gender is one of the primary structures of oppression, and that sexuality is a fundamental mode of exercising domination. And it's an acknowledgement that where power systems affect different people differently, certain issues, such as health and incarceration, take on additional implications when viewed through the lens of gender.

The pieces by Theresa Warburton and by Romina Akemi & Bree Busk provide some questioning of the feminism of anarchism and the anarchism of feminism. Alexander McClelland and Zoë Dodd and Collen Hackett (firehawk) address some of the specific issues.

If anarchism and feminism aren't guaranteed to be synonymous, then what might anarchists and feminists have to offer each other?

It may be (listen, manarchist!) that anarchism still has some things to learn about how to better realize its own ideals and aspirations, from other practitioners of counter-power. For example, in recent history, the roots of many anarchist organizing habits and creative aesthetics can be found in feminist and radical queer political cultures, while many anarchist analyses of power and emancipation have already been brilliantly articulated through the intersectional insights of feminists of color. (Raise your hands, non-cis white men, if you've ever had the experience of being ignored when you offer an idea, only to hear it praised when a man says it. We thought so.)

An anarchist feminism is an argument that heteropatriarchy is best dismantled through a radical attack on all hierarchical systems and structures of oppression and exploitation. A feminist anarchism is an argument that the successful abolition of all hierarchical systems and structures of oppression and exploitation requires antipatriarchal tactics, visions, means and ends. The struggle for a world without domination and injustice continues on all fronts and, when considering the full range of intersectionality, emancipation has not yet fully occurred; anarcha-feminism is needed until all these aspects have been addressed.

On some of the lessons for anarchism from Black and indigenous feminism, see the pieces by Hillary Lazar, and Laura Hall.

Since we're identifying influences and affinities, is there anything like a canonical history of anarcha-feminist practice or theoretical discourse? And if there is, just because we honor our predecessors' crucial contributions thus far, does that mean we can't also push them further? (Would you rather herd anarchists, or cats? We thought so.)

Those who are much known, named and talked about as such are scanty. There's the Enlightenment-era partnership of Mary Wollstonecraft, a woman considered a forebear of feminism, and William Godwin, a man considered a forebear of classical anarchism—a literal marriage of the two philosophies. There's the early-twentieth-century triumvirate of Emma Goldman, Voltairine de Cleyre, and Lucy Parsons, the heroines of Cuban and Japanese insurgence, and then the *Mujeres Libres* of the Spanish Civil War.

Julia Tanenbaum's piece zeroes in on some more recent history.

When *Quiet Rumors* appeared in the late 1970s, following a period of anarchic (if not necessarily anarchist) cultural and sexual revolution, it filled a gap to become a shared touchstone for any anarcha-feminist library. It gathered together some key texts that continue to have relevance: texts that were as historical to our comrade-aunts of a generation ago as they are to us now, as well as texts that were contemporary to them but now historical to us. Because, of course time has passed, during which more voices have gotten out, the conversation has grown cumulatively, newer critiques have been aired, and more waves of political activity and social change have unfurled. So now we engage with these texts of prior generations critically too, marking what they do and don't say, can and can't do. This skimpy canon is necessary but not sufficient. It's part of a dialogue but not the final word. It's now part of our history, but that history hasn't ended and we have to keep the dialogue going, raising new questions.

For a critical assessment of *Quiet Rumors*, recently reprinted by AK Press, see the review by Raeanna Gleason-Salguero. On new additions to the growing discourse, see reviews by Kim Smith, Sara Rahnoma-Galindo, and Kristian Williams.

And finally, the utopian question: Can an anarchist revolution happen without feminism? What would an anarchist society look like that had truly transcended all kinds of gendered power structures, oppressions and exploitations? A society in which all kinds of relationships were equally possible, from polyamory to monogamous pair bonding? In which all kinds of healthy, freely chosen reproductive choices were supported? In which binaristic gender hierarchy could be broken down, while in the process celebrating what's been subordinated and devalued by the construction of that hierarchy? In which alternative structures of family or community existed, not limited to blood kin or nuclear units, to provide for the mutual care of all, at every stage from infancy to the end of life, enabling the multigenerational proliferation of radical countercultures? In which capitalism couldn't extract a double surplus from the unpaid care work and reproductive labor, and the underpaid wage labor, of female workers? In which infinite forms of gender expression and sexuality were available for any body, with no penalization in terms of access to resources, opportunities, respect?

What would it look like if we really no longer needed to specify anarcha-feminism?

# FEMINISM...
# ANARCHISM...
# ANARCHA-
# FEMINISM

## CINDY CRABB

-------------------------

*Cindy Crabb is the author of the long running, political-autobiographical zine* Doris. *She edited the zines* Support, Learning Good Consent, Filling the Void, *and* Masculinities.
*www.dorisdorisdoris.com*

# feminism...

But still, it wasn't quite a big enough framework

# ...anarchism

In a world without domination, we could find out what we really needed and who we really are. Without media and government and corporate control, we could create worlds based on care and connection and mutual aid – from each according to their ability to each according to their need. When people's lives were full of meaning and shared goals, the hatred could be unlearned. No more need for power over others when each person's self was recognized and celebrated and when each being was seen and embraced as part of the larger whole. I loved the vision and the history – the ideas and theories and strategies. I wanted to build counter-institutions and collective organizations and study groups and art and community and action/education/example.

# anarchafeminism

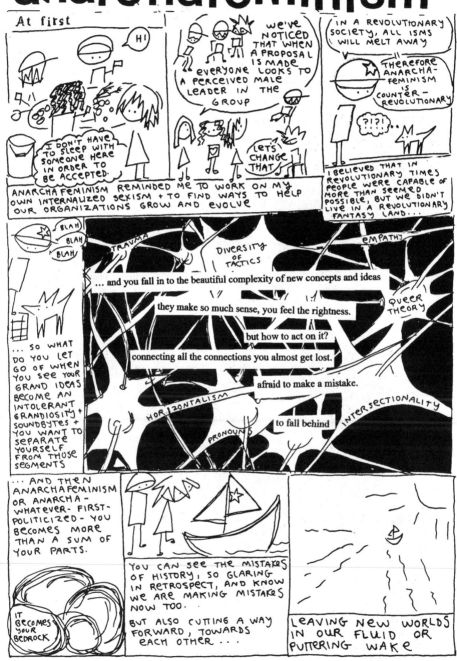

At first

HI

I DON'T HAVE TO SLEEP WITH SOMEONE HERE IN ORDER TO BE ACCEPTED.

WE'VE NOTICED THAT WHEN A PROPOSAL IS MADE EVERYONE LOOKS TO A PERCEIVED MALE LEADER IN THE GROUP

LET'S CHANGE THAT

IN A REVOLUTIONARY SOCIETY, ALL ISMS WILL MELT AWAY

THEREFORE ANARCHA-FEMINISM IS COUNTER-REVOLUTIONARY

?!?!

ANARCHA FEMINISM REMINDED ME TO WORK ON MY OWN INTERNALIZED SEXISM + TO FIND WAYS TO HELP OUR ORGANIZATIONS GROW AND EVOLVE

I BELIEVED THAT IN REVOLUTIONARY TIMES PEOPLE WERE CAPABLE OF MORE THAN SEEMED POSSIBLE, BUT WE DIDN'T LIVE IN A REVOLUTIONARY FANTASY LAND...

BLAH BLAH BLAH

TRAUMA

DIVERSITY OF TACTICS

EMPATHY

... and you fall in to the beautiful complexity of new concepts and ideas

they make so much sense, you feel the rightness.

QUEER THEORY

but how to act on it?

connecting all the connections you almost get lost.

... SO WHAT DO YOU LET GO OF WHEN YOU SEE YOUR GRAND IDEAS BECOME AN INTOLERANT GRANDIOSITY + SOUNDBYTES + YOU WANT TO SEPARATE YOURSELF FROM THOSE SEGMENTS

afraid to make a mistake.

HORIZONTALISM

to fall behind

PRONOUN

INTERSECTIONALITY

... AND THEN ANARCHAFEMINISM OR ANARCHA-WHATEVER- FIRST-POLITICIZED- YOU BECOMES MORE THAN A SUM OF YOUR PARTS.

IT BECOMES YOUR BEDROCK

YOU CAN SEE THE MISTAKES OF HISTORY, SO GLARING IN RETROSPECT, AND KNOW WE ARE MAKING MISTAKES NOW TOO.

BUT ALSO CUTTING A WAY FORWARD, TOWARDS EACH OTHER ...

LEAVING NEW WORLDS IN OUR FLUID OR PUTTERING WAKE

# TO DESTROY DOMINATION IN ALL ITS FORMS:
## ANARCHA-FEMINIST THEORY, ORGANIZATION AND ACTION, 1970-1978

-- -- -- -- -- -- -- --

### JULIA TANENBAUM

As anarchists look for genealogies of principles and praxis in a variety of social movements, from the anarcho-pacifists who spoke out against World War II to anarchists who joined the Black Power movement, so too should they look for their feminist foremothers, not only in the early 20th century anarchist movement but in the radical women's movement of the 1970s. Many radical feminists shared anarchist goals such as ending domination, hierarchy, capitalism, gender roles, and interpersonal violence, and utilized and influenced the key anarchist organizational structure of the small leaderless affinity group. They grappled with the questions of how to balance autonomy and egalitarianism and create nonhierarchical organizations that also promoted personal growth and leadership. In 1974, Lynne Farrow wrote, "Feminism practices what anarchism preaches."[1]

Anarcha-feminism was at first created and defined by women who saw radical feminism itself as anarchistic. In 1970, during the rapid growth of small leaderless consciousness raising (CR) groups around the country, and a corresponding theory of radical feminism that opposed domination, some feminists, usually after discovering anarchism through the writings of Emma Goldman, observed the "intuitive anarchism" of the women's

Art by Bec Young | justseeds.org

liberation movement. Radical feminism emphasized the personal as political, what we would now call prefigurative politics, and a dedication to ending hierarchy and domination, both in theory and practice.[2] CR groups functioned as the central organizational form of the radical feminist movement, and by extension the early anarcha-feminist movement.[3] Members shared their feelings and experiences and realized that their problems were political. The theories of patriarchy they developed explained what women initially saw as personal failures. Consciousness raising was not therapy, as liberal feminists and politicos frequently claimed; its purpose was social transformation, not self-transformation.[4] Radical feminist and anarchist theory and practice share remarkable similarities. In a 1972 article critiquing Rita Mae Brown's calls for a lesbian party, anarchist working-class lesbian feminist Su Katz described how her anarchism came "directly out of" her feminism, and meant decentralization, teaching women to take care of one another, and smashing power relations, all of which were feminist values.[5] Radical feminism attributed domination to the nuclear family structure, which they claimed treats children and women as property and teaches them to obey authority in all aspects of life, and to patriarchal hierarchical thought patterns that encouraged relationships of dominance and submission.[6] To radical feminists and anarcha-feminists, the alternative to domination was sisterhood, which would replace hierarchy and the nuclear family with relationships based on autonomy and equality. A chant that appeared in a 1970 issue of a feminist newspaper read, "We learn the joys of equality/Of relationships

without dominance/Among sisters/We destroy domination in all its forms."[7] These relationships, structured around sisterhood, trust, and friendship, were of particular importance to the radical feminist vision of abolishing hierarchy. As radical feminist theologian Mary Daly wrote in 1973, "The development of sisterhood is a unique threat, for it is directed against the basic social and psychic model of hierarchy and domination."[8] Radical feminists opposed the "male domineering attitude" and "male hierarchical thought patterns," and attempted to act as equals in relationships deeper than male friendships.[9]

To feminists familiar with anarchism, the connections between both radical feminist and anarchist theory and practice were obvious. Anarchist feminism was essentially a step in self-conscious theoretical development, and anarcha-feminists believed that an explicit anarchist analysis, and knowledge of the history of anarchists who faced similar structural and theoretical obstacles, would help women overcome the coercion of elites and create groups structured to be accountable to their members but not hierarchical.[10] They built an independent women's movement and a feminist critique of anarchism, along with an anarchist critique of feminism. To anarcha-feminists, the women's movement represented a new potential for anarchist revolution, for a movement to confront forms of domination and hierarchy, personal and political. Unlike Goldman, Voltairine De Cleyre, the members of Mujeres Libres, and countless other female anarchists concerned with the status of women in the nineteenth and early-twentieth century, they became feminists before they became anarchists.

Anarcha-feminists eventually merged into the anti-nuclear movement by the end of 1978, but not before contributing to crucial movement debates among both anarchists and feminists, building egalitarian, leaderless, empowering alternative institutions, and altering US anarchism in theory and practice.

## BECOMING ANARCHA-FEMINISTS

The term "anarchist-feminist," later used interchangeably with anarcho-feminist and anarcha-feminist, first appeared in an August 1970 issue of the Berkeley-based movement newspaper, *It Ain't Me Babe*. The newspaper published an editorial calling for "feminist anarchist revolution" next to an article about Emma Goldman. The collective did not synthesize a theory of anarcha-feminism, but rather explained how their anarchist beliefs related to the organizational structure of the paper, which they designed as an affinity group to encourage autonomy and discourage "power relationships or leader follower patterns."[11] *It Ain't Me Babe* exemplified the "intuitive anarchism" of the early women's liberation movement. Its masthead read "end all hierarchies" and the paper contained articles like Ellen Leo's "Power Trips," which exemplified the radical feminist tendency to oppose all forms of domination. Leo wrote in 1970, "The oppression of women is not an isolated phenomenon. It is but one of the many forms of domination in this society. It is a basic belief that one person or group of people has the right to subjugate, rule and boss others."[12] Like anarchists, these feminists connected the oppression of women to a larger phenomenon of domination. Beginning in 1968 and growing in

strength until 1972, radical feminism was anything but monolithic and many participants differed greatly in regards to their views on sexuality, the family, the state, organizational structure, and the inclusion of transgender women in the movement.

Most anarcha-feminists were initially radicalized by the political and cultural milieu of the anti-war movement, but it was their experiences in the women's liberation movement combined with the influence of Emma Goldman that led them to develop anarcha-feminism as a strategy. As feminists struggled to reclaim women's history, Goldman became a feminist icon due to her advocacy of birth control, free love, and personal freedom. In 1971 radical feminist novelist and historian Alix Kates Shulman wrote, "Emma Goldman's name has re-emerged from obscurity to become a veritable password of radical feminism. Her works rose from the limbo of being out of print to...being available in paperback. Her face began appearing on T-shirts, her name on posters, her words on banners."[13] Goldman criticized the bourgeois feminist movement and its goal of suffrage, which led many women to criticize her as a "man's woman." However, Shulman and many others argued that Goldman was a radical feminist worthy of recognition because she stressed the oppression of women as women by the institutions of the patriarchal family and puritan morality, as well as religion and the state.[14] As anarcha-feminist Cathy Levine wrote in 1974, "The style, the audacity of Emma Goldman, has been touted by women who do not regard themselves as anarchists... because Emma was so right-on.... It is no accident, either, that the anarchist Red Terror named Emma was also an advocate and practitioner of free-love; she was an affront to more capitalist shackles than any of her Marxist contemporaries."[15] Feminists honored Goldman's ideas and legacy by opening an Emma Goldman Clinic for Women in Iowa in 1973, publishing new volumes of her work, naming their theater troupes after her, and writing screenplays, operas, and stage plays about her life.[16] In 1970, the women's liberation periodical *Off Our Backs* dedicated an issue to Goldman with her image on the cover. Despite this, Betsy Auleta and Bobbie Goldstone's article about Goldman's life discussed what they perceived as her faults (her opposition to suffrage and disconnect from much of the women's movement) because she had become a "super-heroine" in the movement.[17]

## SIREN AND EARLY ANARCHA-FEMINIST NETWORKS

Goldman encouraged women to make connections between radical feminism and anarchism, and her writings often served as radical feminists' introduction to anarchism or the impetus for them to make connections between anarchism and feminism. To many anarcha-feminists this theory represented both a critique of the sexism of the male New Left, including its anarchist members, as well as a critique of socialist and liberal feminism. Despite this intuitive anarchism, attempts by early anarcha-feminists to develop an anarchist analysis within many radical feminist collectives felt silenced, while women in the anarchist movement, where misogyny ruled as much as in the rest of the New Left, also felt alienated. Anarcha-feminist

attempts to elucidate connections between feminism and anarchism, like those of Arlene Meyers and Evan Paxton, were often met with intimidation and censorship in mixed groups. These conditions created the possibility for an independent anarcha-feminist movement, but first, anarcha-feminists would have to communicate and develop their theories.

Early anarcha-feminist theory and debate emerged through *Siren* newsletter. The first issue, produced as a journal in 1971, contained "Who We Are: The Anarcho-Feminist Manifesto," written by Arlene Wilson, a member of the Chicago Anarcho-Feminist Collective.[18] The manifesto focused on differentiating anarcha-feminism from socialist feminism through a critique of the state: "The intelligence of womankind has at last been brought to bear on such oppressive male inventions as the church and the legal family; it must now be brought to re-evaluate the ultimate stronghold of male domination, the State."[19]

In February of 1970 Arlene Meyers and the *Siren* collective switched from journal to newsletter format, which allowed feminists throughout the US to participate in defining anarcha-feminism and its theory.[20] *Siren* allowed women in diverse (often not explicitly anarchist) collectives in many regions of the country to communicate and develop their theory. Later issues of the newsletter included news items related to feminist and anarchist activism, including political prisoner support for anarchists in Spain through the Anarchist Black Cross, women's health clinics, childcare and living collectives, and working at infoshops like Mother Earth Bookstore.[21]

The last three issues of *Siren*,

published in 1973, contain the majority of the newsletter's analysis and debate, covering topics such as state power and authoritarianism, prefigurative politics, lesbian feminism, and gender identity and expression. Issue 10 of *Siren* contained two statements by transgender individuals, critiquing both sexism and the gender binary, and offering a progressive vision of transgender inclusion within the movement. Eden W, a member of the Tucson Anarcho-Feminists, described her experiences as a "male woman" and critiqued "the authoritarianism that demands that males must be of one gender and females of another," thus critiquing the gender binary itself as a form of authoritarianism.[22] Finally, she asked feminists to look on "femmiphiles" as their sisters.[23]

This essay stood in contrast with the prejudice towards trans women in the larger radical feminist movement, which sometimes portrayed them as interlopers who brought male privilege into women only spaces. That same year radical feminist Robin Morgan famously denounced male to female transgender feminist songwriter and activist Beth Elliot as a rapist and "infiltrator" at the 1973 West Coast Lesbian Conference, although it is worth noting that two-thirds of the conference-goers voted for Elliot to stay.[24] Some feminists conflated transgender women with men in drag, accused them of being rapists, and felt that they retained male privilege and should not be allowed in feminist spaces.[25] Although anarcha-feminists were undoubtedly influenced by this discourse, attitudes towards transgender people were not monolithic in the feminist movement at large. Eden W's statement emphasizes that she is heterosexual, perhaps because of this widespread fear of transgender women as

rapist infiltrators. This limited discussion of transsexuality nevertheless reveals that anarcha-feminists were willing to discuss this conflict, and give transgender people a voice in the movement.

Issue 8 of *Siren* also contained "Blood of the Flower," a statement written by Marian Leighton and Cathy Levine, members of the Cambridge based Black Rose Anarcho-Feminist collective.[26] Unlike Wilson, Leighton and Levine reject not only socialist feminism's analysis of the state, but its tactics and the idea of movement building altogether. To them, "movements," as represented by the male Left and its ideas of a vanguard, separated politics from personal dreams of liberation until women abandoned their dreams or dropped out of the movement altogether. Instead, they advocated leaderless affinity groups in which each member could act as an individual, and presented this anarchist form of organization as the alternative to hierarchical movement politics practiced by socialist feminists and liberal feminists. The small leaderless affinity group allows members to participate "on an equal level of power" without leadership determining the direction of the movement.[27] They wrote, "Organizing women, in the New Left and Marxist left, is viewed as amassing troops for the Revolution. But we affirm that each woman joining in struggle is the Revolution."[28] This anarcha-feminist vision, almost similar to the cell-like structure of earlier insurrectionary anarchist groups, emphasized valuing individual contributions in small groups instead of building the large, often authoritarian, and impersonal "revolutionary armies" that many New Leftists and socialist feminists envisioned. To achieve this, anarcha-feminists would build their movement through small affinity groups and participating in various feminist and anarchist counter-institutions.

## SMALL GROUPS, GROWING NETWORKS

Anarcha-feminists formed study groups, which, like the CR groups, also acted as affinity groups, and formed and dissolved quickly. Many groups were located in university towns, partially due to the success of AnarchoFeminist Network Notes as a communications network, which allowed activists to communicate and organize outside of major urban areas. Collectives were often small, flexible, and project-based. Because they required intimacy and small size, when groups became too large, as the Des Moines and Cambridge based Black Rose Anarcho-Feminists did, they split into multiple study and action groups.[29] These groups also acted as affinity groups that collectively participated in action around various local and national issues, from the local food co-op to international political prisoner support to the lesbian movement to ecology struggles and the anti-nuclear movement.[30]

The collective Tiamat originated in Ithaca, New York in 1975 and dissolved in 1978. Their name originated from the tale of a goddess of chaos and creation, feared by men but worshipped by women.[31] The collective read anarchist theory together, shared ideas, and put out an issue of the newsletter *Anarcha-Feminist Notes* in 1977. According to former member Elaine Leeder's reflections, the collective members participated in political activities ranging from protesting the building of a local shopping mall to raising money for a day care center for political dissidents

in Chile. Furthermore, Leeder argued that the collective was a functioning "anarchistic society": "We are leaderless, non-hierarchical…and always ready to change. We live self-management, learn what it is together…and support each other."[32] Tiamat supported Leeder's interest in the mental health liberation movement and her successful effort to stop the introduction of electro-shock therapy at a local mental hospital.[33]

Anarcha-feminists worked in a wide variety of movements, and thus brought their prefigurative and feminist ideas to a diverse audience. Furthermore, a focus on education allowed anarcha-feminists to develop their own autonomy and talents. However, these diverse activities and the ephemeral nature of these collectives illustrate why anarcha-feminism is almost always ignored by historians and documents or records of these collectives are difficult to find.

To unite a small, decentralized movement, anarcha-feminists created communications networks through newsletters and conferences. At the Yellow Springs Socialist Feminist Conference in Ohio in 1975, the future members of Tiamat met and anarcha-feminists proposed that they should combine their networks and mailing lists.[34] After the conference, anarcha-feminists established new collectives in Bloomington, Illinois, and Buffalo, New York.[35] The conference was considered notable for its lack of a definition of socialist feminism, and its broad "principles of unity" included two items associated with radical feminism and anarcha-feminism, but condemned by male socialists: recognizing the need for an autonomous women's movement, and that all oppression is interrelated.[36]

Its broad principles illustrated how socialist feminists viewed economic oppression as one of many forms of domination rather than as the "lynchpin," as male Marxists tended to argue. Similar in format to *Siren*, *Anarcha-Feminist Notes* originated from a merger of two short-lived newsletters, *Anarcho-Feminist Network Notes* and *The Anarchist-Feminist Communications Network*.[37] A different collective published each issue of the newsletter, and thus each varied in style and content. The Des Moines anarcha-feminist study and action group, Tiamat, and the Utopian Feminists were among the collectives who published issues of the newsletter. Although the last issue was published in March 1978, *Anarcha-Feminist Notes*, while it existed, acted as an effective means of communication for a decentralized movement.

Prior to Tiamat's dissolution, it sponsored an Anarcha-Feminist Conference in June 1978 that attracted women from London, Italy, Toronto, and several US cities.[38] In an idyllic location in Ithaca, women attended three days of workshops on topics such as anarcha-feminism and unions, self-liberation as social change, the ecology movement and anarcha-feminism, women and violence, building the anarcha-feminist network, matriarchy and feminist spirituality, beards and body hair, combatting racism, and anarcha-feminism and class.[39] The conference's theme was "Anarcha-Feminism: Growing Stronger," which referenced the growth of anarcha-feminist theory and action since its inception. A packet given to conference attendees contained an essay called Tribes by Martha Courtot, which echoed conference goers' feelings about building anarcha-feminist community. "We tell you this: we are doing the impossible. We are teaching ourselves to be human. When we are finished, the strands which connect us will be unbreakable; already we are stronger than we ever have been."[40] Unlike purely cultural feminism, anarcha-feminists connected this strength and community to a larger fight against domination. Both their personal lives and organizing efforts in mixed movements like the ecology movement were important parts of their politics.

## FROM CONSCIOUSNESS-RAISING TO COUNTER-INSTITUTIONS

Historian Barbara Ryan argues that the "small group sector" of the feminist movement virtually disappeared by the mid 1970s, due to ideological and practical conflicts within the movement and the influence of liberal feminists, who advocated larger structured organizations.[41] However this frequent narrative, which emphasizes the fast rise and fall of small CR groups, negates the crucial contributions of anarcha-feminists, who continued to organize within small, decentralized, and leaderless feminist collectives throughout the 1970s. Radical feminists extended the CR group's anarchistic structure to a variety of other projects, such as domestic violence shelters, living collectives, and periodicals, many of which continued to support women through the late 1970s and into the 1980s. According to Helen Ellenbogen's 1977 review of anarcha-feminist groups, many of these collectives were not explicitly anarchist but "intuitively anarchist," such as the grassroots domestic violence shelters in Cambridge and Los

Angeles where anarcha-feminists worked and observed practices like discouraging women from calling the police to deal with abusive males.[42] Ellenbogen remarks on how anarcha-feminists joined women's health clinics in Los Angeles, Seattle, and Boston, which resisted cooperation with the state and utilized collective process.[43] In a 1972 article in *Siren*, Los Angeles anarcha-feminist Evan Paxton explained the anarcha-feminist principles of these self-help clinics, including the one where she worked. Clinics gave "women the confidence and knowledge to take care of their own bodies, which is essential in the struggle for self control."[44] Women's health clinics helped women avoid the paternalism of (usually male) doctors and gain self-control.[45]

Anarcha-feminists operated a free school in Baltimore, which taught courses on Wilhelm Reich, movement structural skills, how to form a co-op, and anarchist and feminist political theory.[46] Others worked on media projects like feminist newspapers or journals such as *Through the Looking Glass*, which focused on women prisoners, *The Second Wave*, and feminist radio stations.[47] This focus on outreach and education illustrates anarcha-feminists' long-term approach to revolution. Theorists like Kornegger and Rebecca Staton argued that anarchist revolution, both historically and in the present, requires preparation through education, the creation of alternative nonhierarchical structures, changes in consciousness, and direct action.[48] As Staton wrote in a 1975 article in *Anarcho-Feminist Network Notes*, "Anarchists…have seen their own role in the revolutionary process as agitators and educators—not as vanguard…. The Revolution, for Anarchists, is the transformation of society by people

taking direct control of their own lives."[49] In 1976, in the first issue of *Anarcha-Feminist Notes*, Judi Stein, an anarcha-feminist who worked at a feminist health center, described her experiences with collective processes, self-help, and feminism there as "ways to live out anarchism."[50] By working at self-help clinics, free schools, feminist radio stations, newspapers, and domestic violence shelters, anarcha-feminists spread their ideas and organizational methods, and helped themselves and other women in their own struggles for autonomy.

The self-described gay anarcho-feminist printer Come! Unity Press explicitly connected their political philosophy to their organizational structure. Founded in 1972, the press published *Anarchism: The Feminist Connection*, feminist writings of Emma Goldman, an issue of *Anarcho-Feminist Notes*, and other classic anarchist writings, like the speeches of Sacco and Vanzetti.[51] Notably, they allowed members to decide for themselves how much they could afford to pay for the use of their printing facilities, which exemplified their anarcha-feminist philosophy of "survival by sharing." The women of the press wrote in 1976, "As anarcho-feminists we want to end all forms of domination. Money is a…tool of power. It is a means of enforcing racism, sexism, or starvation and control over basic survival."[52] In a 1976 article critiquing "feminist businesses" in *The Second Wave*, Peggy Kornegger praised this model, and wrote that the press's "'survival by sharing'…certainly demonstrates if nothing else, that there are ways of confronting capitalism that don't involve either power or control—and that work!"[53] This alternative economic model helped the feminist movement, and its own members, survive.

## "ANARCHO-SEXISM" AND ANARCHA-FEMINIST INTERACTION WITH THE ANTI-CAPITALIST LEFT

Anarcha-feminists also worked within the larger anarchist movement, attending anarchist conferences and confronting sexism in mixed groups. Anarcha-feminists attended the Anarchs-of-New-York-sponsored Live and Let Live Festival in April 1974. Anarcha-feminist groups like the New York Anarcho-Feminists and Come! Unity Press participated along with several hundred other conference goers, and the final schedule included four anarcha-feminist workshops amongst many other unscheduled lesbian and anarcha-feminist discussions and meet-ups. The feminist periodical *Off Our Backs* included a report on the conference written by two anarcha-feminists, Mecca Reliance and Jean Horan.[54] Reliance, who attended both mixed and impromptu women-only workshops on anarcha-feminism, wrote that the mixed workshop was uninteresting and focused on the abolition of the nuclear family, apparently the only comfortable topic for the many male attendees, while the women-only workshop was energetic and facilitated a focus on organization and internal process.[55] This mirrored one impetus towards separatism in the radical feminist movement: male-dominated meetings in the New Left led women to censor their thoughts and long for an environment where they could speak freely and determine their own agenda.[56] Anarcha-feminists also attended the 1975 Midwest Anarchist Conference, and experienced several incidents of sexism, such as a man trying to take a hammer away from Karen Johnson, assuming that she could not use it because of her gender. However, the man eventually accepted her and other women's criticism of his actions.[57]

Anarcha-feminists experienced sexism in the Industrial Workers of the World (IWW) meetings, and conflicts over sexism in anarchist periodicals like the *Social Revolutionary Anarchist Federation Bulletin* and *The Match* confirmed that many male anarchists shared the sexist attitudes of their Marxist counterparts.[58] These attitudes encouraged separatism, but some anarcha-feminists worked in mixed collectives. Grant Purdy, a member of the Des Moines anarcha-feminist The New World Collective, which existed from 1973-76, wrote an article about her group's experience in a mixed anarchist group called the Redwing Workers Organization (RWO) in the Spring 1977 issue of Anarcha-Feminist Notes.[59] RWO focused on healthcare organizing, but the women in the group pushed feminist perspectives and led the group to treat personal struggles as political ones.[60] She argued that despite frustrations, women could thrive in mixed groups if they created separate women's groups outside of the larger organization, as the Des Moines women did. Women in mixed anarchist organizations taught male anarchists about their own misogyny and learned new skills from their comrades.[61] However, for anarcha-feminists like Purdy, "involvement with men has always been conditional. Men are clear that they are not a priority for us over other women."[62] These separate women's support groups and their presence at conferences illustrate how anarcha-feminists brought their ideas and organizational styles to the male anarchist movement as the radical feminist movement declined.

## DIFFERING FEMINISMS

From the beginning of the movement, anarcha-feminists differentiated socialist feminists and their theories from the traditional male socialist Left. In a 1971 article in the first issue of *Siren*, Arlene Wilson's Chicago-based anarcha-feminist group emphasized that anarcho-feminists "are all socialists" and "refuse to give up this pre-Marxist term," and continued, "We love our Marxist sisters…and have no interest in disassociating ourselves from their constructive struggles." In 1974 Black Rose anarcha-feminist Marian Leighton commented that socialist feminist literature is not "narrowly dogmatic or opportunistic"[63] like that of traditional male Marxists. Rather, it could be included in anarcha-feminist analysis. Anarcha-feminist filmmaker Lizzie Borden argued in a 1977 article in feminist art journal Heresies that Marxist women like Rosa Luxemburg, Alexandra Kollantai, and Angelica Balabanoff came closer to anarchism in their opposition to bureaucracy, authoritarianism, and the subversion of the revolution by the Bolsheviks than their male comrades.[64] However, like Leighton, she emphasized that these anarchistic tendencies stemmed from socialization and lack of access to power, not simple essentialist understandings of gender. As Carol Ehrlich wrote in her 1977 article *Socialism, Anarchism, and Feminism*, which appealed to socialist and radical feminists to embrace anarchism, "Women of all classes, races, and life circumstances have been on the receiving end of domination too long to want to exchange one set of masters for another."[65] Leighton, Kronneger, and Ehrlich argued the defining

distinction between radical feminism and anarcha-feminism was largely a step in self-conscious theoretical development.[66] Thus, it was feminists' unfamiliarity with anarchism that led them to embrace Marxism, although their ideology, "skeptical of any social theory that comes with a built-in set of leaders and followers" held more in common with anarchism.[67]

Anarcha-Feminists and socialist feminists often found their common interests outweighed their ideological differences, and worked together. Arlene Wilson was also a member of the socialist feminist group the Chicago Women's Liberation Union (CWLU), along with other antiauthoritarian women.[68] Wilson introduced Penny Pixler and other CWLU women to the Chicago chapter of the newly reconstituted IWW in the early 70s.[69] They found the Chicago IWW less patriarchal and hierarchical than many Marxist parties and sects and were impressed with its history of women organizers. Several joined the union and became active in the Chicago Branch in addition to their continued work with CWLU projects.[70] The CWLU dissolved acrimoniously in 1976 due to internal conflict over what some members observed as the group's white middle-class orientation. Pixler and other former members shifted their primary activity to the IWW. Pixler contributed many articles to the *Industrial Worker* focusing on women workers, and contributed an article about the position of women in Maoist China to anarcha-feminist literary journal *Whirlwind* in 1978.[71]

Anarcha-Feminists were also influenced by the theories of the French situationists, who positioned women's oppression as a part of larger systems of power relations without reducing it to an effect of capitalism. Carol Ehrlich and Lynne Farrow argued that Situationism should be a component of anarcha-feminist analysis because it emphasizes both an awareness of capitalist oppression and the need to transform everyday life.[72] Situationists expanded Marx's theories of alienation and commodity fetishism to apply to modern consumer capitalism and argued that capitalist society led to the increasing tendency towards the consumption of social relations and identity through commodities and alienated people from all aspects of their lives, not just their labor.[73] In her 1977 article *Socialism, Anarchism, and Feminism*, Ehrlich argued that a Situationist analysis is applicable to anarcha-feminist theory. With a Situationist analysis, all women's oppression is real, despite their class status. Furthermore, women held a special relationship to the commodity economy as both consumers and objects to be consumed by men. Ehrlich argued "A Situationist analysis ties consumption of economic goods to consumption of ideological goods, and then tells us to create situations (guerrilla actions on many levels) that will break that pattern of socialized acceptance of the world as it is."[74]

Historian Alice Echols argued that after 1975 cultural feminism eclipsed radical feminism, and fundamentally depoliticized it. She wrote, "Radical feminism was a political movement dedicated to eliminating the sex-class system, whereas cultural feminism was a countercultural movement aimed at reversing the cultural valuation of the male and the devaluation of the female."[75] Echols argued that feminists embraced cultural feminism because they could not deal with their differences in race, class, and sexuality, and it became easier to subsume them under universal ideals of womanhood. Anarcha-feminism embraced elements of cultural feminism, but rejected its apolitical aspects and the popular matriarchy theories pioneered by Elizabeth Gould Davis, Jane Alpert, Phyllis Chesler, and Mary Daly.[76] These essentialist theories argued that the negative valuation of femininity rather than femininity itself should be challenged, and that power in the hands of women, rather than men, could lead to a feminist society. For example, Jane Alpert's influential manifesto Mother Right argued that women's potential for motherhood made them different from, but superior to, men.

Ehrlich critiqued "spirituality trippers" and the Amazon Nation for being out of touch with the reality of political and economic oppression, and for failing to recognize that all power, whether in the hands of women or men, is coercive, but other anarcha-feminists saw positive aspects of cultural feminism.[77] Cathy Levine defended cultural projects and argued that "creating a woman's culture is the means through which we shall restore our lost humanity."[78] To Levine and other anarcha-feminists, notably Peggy Kornegger (who crafted a theory of anarcha-feminist spirituality), anarcha-feminism embraced both the cultural and political. As many former feminists embraced spirituality gurus and their pacifying, depoliticizing, and anti-feminist programs, Kornegger argued that feminists must embrace both the feminist spirituality of theorists such as Mary Daly and physical and political resistance. Her 1976 article

"The Spirituality Ripoff" in *The Second Wave* argued for a feminist approach to spirituality which emphasized both personal growth and political action. Kornegger wrote, "We need no longer separate being and action into two categories. It means that we need no longer call ourselves 'cultural feminists' or 'political feminists' but must see ourselves as both....It means teaching ourselves womancraft and self-defense."[79] Describing this realization as a revolutionary "leap of consciousness," Kornegger positioned anarcha-feminism as the next stage of consciousness raising which would mend the divides between spirituality and politics and between groups of feminists.

Anarcha-feminists combined aspects of radical, cultural, and socialist feminism, but added a critique of domination itself. Unlike socialist feminists, they saw nonhierarchical structures as "essential to feminist practice."[80] Both radical and anarchist feminists dedicated themselves to building prefigurative institutions, a task socialist feminists did not always see as a vital part of their revolutionary program.[81] While cultural feminists often rejected "male theory" and their roots in the New Left in favor of a depoliticized approach to feminism, anarcha-feminists combined emphasis on building a women's culture with a strong theoretical perspective and class consciousness. Constantly learning from other feminists and adjusting anarcha-feminist theory accordingly, rather than dogmatism, was a crucial feature of anarcha-feminism and part of the reason anarcha-feminists participated in such a variety of movements. Su Negrin wrote that "no political umbrella can cover all my needs" while Kornegger argued that it was crucial to break down

barriers between feminists. As she wrote in 1976, "Although I call myself an anarcha-feminist, this definition can easily include socialism, communism, cultural feminism, lesbian separatism, or any of a dozen other political labels."[82] Anarcha-feminists learned from women in other parts of the feminist movement, despite their disagreements.

## THE TYRANNY OF STRUCTURELESSNESS OR THE TYRANNY OF TYRANNY

The movement's debate over structure and leadership gave the new anarcha-feminist position relevance and strategic value. An anarchistic commitment to equality and friendship structured feminist political organizations and fostered egalitarianism and respect, and reinforced mutual knowledge and trust, but when groups became clique-like and elites emerged, feminists utilized various structural methods to ensure equality.[83] Radical feminist groups utilized lot systems to distribute tasks in an egalitarian manner, disc systems that ensured equal speaking time by distributing an equal amount of discs to members at the beginning of the meeting and instructing them to give one up each time they spoke, and collective decision-making through consensus or other means.[84] They viewed women's capacities as equal but stymied by their socialization, and empowered thousands of women to write, speak in public, talk to the press, chair a meeting, and make decisions for the first time.[85]

However, the goals of empowerment and egalitarianism came into conflict.[86] "Elites", or women with informal leadership positions within groups, often socially coerced other women into agreeing with them, or not stating their opinions at all, and in reaction the movement developed a paranoia about elites; women who exercised leadership or even attempted to teach skills to other members were often shunned and trashed.[87] This triggered bitter statements like Anselma dell'Olio's 1970 speech, "Divisiveness and Self-Destruction in the Women's Movement: A Letter of Resignation," which claimed, "If you are...an achiever you are immediately labeled...a ruthless mercenary, out to get her fame and fortune over the dead bodies of selfless sisters who have buried their abilities and sacrificed their ambitions for the greater glory of Feminism."[88] Ironically, to some women, this justified the behavior of women who were in fact dominating others, and then presented themselves as tragic heroines destroyed by their envious and less talented "sisters."[89]

In her widely read 1970 article, Jo Freeman, going by the pen name Joreen, argued that not only feminists' personal practices, but the "tyranny of structurelessness" limited democracy and that to overcome it, groups needed to create explicit structures accountable to their membership.[90] After circulating widely among feminists, the paper was published in the feminist journal *The Second Wave* in 1972. To Freeman, structure was inevitable because of individuals' differing talents, predispositions, and backgrounds, but became pernicious when unacknowledged.[91] Leaders were appointed as spokespeople by the media, and structurelessness often disguised informal, unacknowledged, and unaccountable leadership and hierarchies within groups. Thus,

Freeman argued that structure would prevent elites from emerging and ensure democratic decision-making. Some anarcha-feminists, such as Carol Ehrlich agreed with this part of Freeman's analysis while others, like Cathy Levine and Marian Leighton, opposed structure entirely.[92] However, Joreen also decried the small group's size and emphasis on consciousness raising as ineffective, and advocated for large organizations.[93] Even after calling for "diffuse, flexible, open, and temporary" leadership, Freeman argued that to successfully fight patriarchy, the movement must move beyond the small groups of its consciousness-raising phase and shift to large, usually hierarchical, organizations.[94]

Anarcha-Feminists asserted that the small group was not simply a reaction to male hierarchical organization, but a solution to the movement's problems with both structure and leadership. In 1974, Cathy Levine, the cowriter of "Blood of the Flower," wrote the anarcha-feminist response to Freeman, "The Tyranny of Tyranny." Often printed with Freeman's essay, Levine's piece first appeared in the anarchist journal *Black Rose*.[95] Levine argued that feminists who utilize the "movement building" strategies of the male Left forgot the importance of the personal as political, psychological oppression, and prefigurative politics. Instead of building large, alienating, and hierarchical organizations, feminists should continue to utilize small groups which "multiply the strength of each member" by developing their skills and relationships in a nurturing non-hierarchical environment.[96] Building on the theories of Wilhelm Reich, she argued that psychological repression kept women from confronting capitalism and patriarchy, and thus caused the problem of elites.[97] Developing small groups and a women's culture would invigorate individual women and prevent burn out, but also create a prefigurative alternative to hierarchical organization. She wrote, "The reason for building a movement on a foundation of collectives is that we want to create a revolutionary culture consistent with our view of the new society; it is more than a reaction; the small group is a solution."[98]

Similarly, Carol Ehrlich, Su Negrin, and Lynne Farrow argued that the small group allowed individuals to fight oppression in their everyday lives.[99] All oppression involved individual actors, even if they acted as an agent of the state or the ruling class. Su Negrin, a member of Murray Bookchin's Anarchos group and radical feminists, wrote and published *Begin At Start* in 1972.[100] Negrin argued that the root structures of domination lie in everyday life because we are dominated but also dominate others, especially in sexual relationships and parenting, and applied this theory to her own life and relationships with her husband and children. These ideas reflected the feminist emphasis on the personal as political and pointing out domination in everyday life. Mutual trust in small groups helps people recognize and work with stylistic differences rather than trying to eliminate them. Similarly, Sue Katz, an anarchist lesbian leader of the working-class feminist Stick it in the Wall Motherfucker collective, responded to Rita Mae Brown's calls for a lesbian party in a May 1972 issue of *The Furies*, claiming that small groups were actually efficient and could deal more effectively with internal problems.[101] The small group emphasized the personal as political and developing relationships

instead of the national campaign related strategy of liberal feminists and some socialist feminist groups.

Levine's individualist focus starkly challenges the emphasis on conformity to ensure egalitarianism in many groups.[102] An anarcha-feminist understanding of equality, rather, would allow women to excel in different areas, provided they teach others the skills. Indeed, much anarcha-feminist work was educational and theorists like Kornegger focused on political education as a crucial area of tactics. As she argued in *Anarchism: The Feminist Connection*, women's intuitive anarchism and egalitarianism was counteracted by socialization in an authoritarian society, but anarchist history and theory provided useful precedent for creating egalitarian-structured organizations that also ensured leadership development and individual autonomy. Kornegger cited the example of the achievements of the anarchist organizations CNT-FAI and the collectives during the Spanish Civil War as an example of "the realization of basic human ideals: freedom, individual creativity, and collective cooperation."[103]

Historically, anarchists grappled with the same questions of structure, organization, and prefiguration feminists were debating. These examples of political education and fluid structures that rotated tasks and leadership would help feminists watch for elites without resorting to voting or hierarchical models of organization.

## NO GODS, NO MASTERS, NO NUKES

As the antinuclear movement emerged and gained strength through the Seabrook nuclear power plant occupation, and later the 1979 Three

Mile Island nuclear meltdown incident, anarcha-feminists shifted their activity to large mixed-gender coalitions of affinity groups.[104] Many anarcha-feminists who attended the 1978 Anarcha-Feminism: Growing Stronger conference sponsored by TIAMAT met up at the Seabrook antinuclear demonstrations, which attracted thousands to participate in nonviolent civil disobedience to occupy the plant.[105] Tellingly, when Tiamat eventually dissolved, members joined a women's anti-nuclear affinity group, the Lesbian Alliance, and others worked with a mixed group on ecology issues.[106] Although they usually participated in women-only affinity groups, they interacted with men and authoritarian male politics in the larger movement. Anarcha-feminists also formed collectives in universities like Hunter College, Cornell, and Wesleyan.[107] Often influenced by the writings of Murray Bookchin, who advocated political study groups, these affinity groups became the primary organizational model of the anti-nuclear direct action movement just as the similarly structured small group was the organizational model of the radical feminist movement.[108]

Throughout the 1980s, anarchist feminists connected the ideas they formed in the women's liberation movement to an even wider range of issues, including violence against women, environmental destruction, militarism, and the nuclear arms race.[109] Roxanne Dunbar-Ortiz argues in the introduction to *Quiet Rumors* that the anarcha-feminist movement "had to all intents and purposes ceased to function" by 1980 as liberal feminists eclipsed radicals and male anarchists remained "traditional" in their sexism.[110] However, even as anarcha-feminists shifted from focusing primarily on women's oppression to a wider array of political issues, the organizational form and process, and the concern with both the personal and political remained. Consensus decision-making, a hallmark of prefigurative politics, was referred to as "feminist process" in the antinuclear movement, illustrating the influence of the many anarcha-feminist affinity groups and other feminists.[111]

However, it remains to be seen if replacing a separate women's movement of small affinity groups with often mixed-gender affinity groups was strategic. Today, many anarchist women and queer people, often in reaction to the sexism of anarchist men and rape culture inside anarchist collectives and movements, are forming their own affinity groups once again. It is worth investigating how changing ideas about gender and sexuality and the rise of queer and trans politics affected this change, and if it is a strategic one. How did theories of intersectionality and Black feminism interact with anarcha-feminism, and differ from earlier anarcha-feminist arguments that often did not directly address racial politics? The history of anarcha-feminism points to these and many more questions in an area of anarchist politics and theory that is generally under-investigated.

## CONCLUSION

Often, anarcha-feminists remarked that women were "natural anarchists" and positioned feminists as an untapped revolutionary force. However, neither the women's movement nor the women in it always acted anarchistically. As activist Kytha Kurin wrote in 1980, "If anarchist tendencies within the feminist movement are accepted as a natural by-product of being female, it puts an unfair pressure on women to 'live up to their natural anarchism' and limits our potential for political development….Many women's groups do disintegrate, many women do exploit other women and men."[112] Radical feminists functioned as anarchists in anarchist spaces while lacking knowledge of anarchism. I think this proves the power of prefigurative politics and liberated anarchist spaces and organizations, free of the unnatural hierarchies that the white supremacist capitalist patriarchy forces upon us, to bring out the "intuitive anarchism" of a variety of people from white middle-class feminists to Occupy Wall Street protestors.[113] Whether their relationships are based on sisterhood, ecology, or race or class solidarity, people have tried, and sometimes failed, to live without dominance and hierarchy. Once radical feminism was, as Kornegger wrote, "the connection that links anarchism to the future."[114] We must look for similar links in our movements today; we can see them throughout what anarchist scholar and activist Chris Dixon termed the antiauthoritarian current, from the prison abolition movement, to the radical environmental movement, to queer and feminist struggles today.[115] If another world is possible, we can and must create it now.

## NOTES

1    Peggy Kornegger, "Anarchism: The Feminist Connection," in *Reinventing Anarchy: What Are Anarchists Thinking These Days?*, ed. Howard Ehrlich (Routledge and Kegan Paul Books, 1979).

2    Prefigurative politics is the desire is to embody, within a movement's political and social practices, the forms of social

relations, decision-making, culture, and human experience that are the ultimate goal. Although anarcha-feminists did not use this language, various scholars have applied it to the women's movement and the New Left. See Sheila Rowbotham, "The Women's Movement and Organizing for Socialism," in *Beyond The Fragments: Feminism and the Making of Socialism*, ed. Sheila Rowbotham, Lynne Segal, and Hilary Wainwright. (London: Merlin Press, 1979), 21-155, and Francesca Polletta, *Freedom Is an Endless Meeting: Democracy in American Social Movements* (Chicago: University Of Chicago Press, 2004). Anarcha-feminists frequently used language like "living the revolution" and "living out anarchism" to describe these practices. See Andrew Cornell, *Unruly Equality: U.S. Anarchism in the Twentieth Century* (Oakland: University of California Press, 2016) on anarchist prefigurative politics during this period.

3    Wini Breines, *The Trouble between Us: An Uneasy History of White and Black Women in the Feminist Movement* (Oxford: Oxford University Press, 2006), 92.

4    Alice Echols, *Daring to Be Bad: Radical Feminism in America, 1967-1975* (Minneapolis: University of Minnesota Press, 1989), 72.

5    Sue Katz, "An Anarchist Plebe Fights Back," *The Furies* 1, no. 4 (n.d.): 12. Rainbow History Online Archives.

6    Wini Breines, *The Trouble Between Us*, 90.

7    "It Ain't Me Babe—A Struggle for Identity," *It Ain't Me Babe*, June 8, 1970. (New York University: Wagner Labor Archives), 11.

8    Mary Daly, *Beyond God the Father: Toward a Philosophy of Women's Liberation* (Beacon Press, 1973), 133.

9    Polletta, *Freedom Is an Endless Meeting*, 162.

10    Although today radical feminism is associated with trans-exclusive feminists, during the 1970s it referred to a wider movement which asserted that gender, not class or race, was the primary contradiction

and that all other forms of social domination originated with male supremacy. The "radical" served to differentiate it from liberal feminism, which focused solely on formal equality and ignored the fundamental problem of fighting for equality in an inherently unjust society. It also referred to the roots of radical feminists in the Marxist and sometimes anarchist New Left, where they experienced sexism that led them to reject the "male movement" and start their own, without the interference of their male oppressors. Radical feminists also differentiated themselves from "politicos," women working in male dominated Leftist groups where the struggle against male supremacy was neglected. [See Echols, *Daring To Be Bad.*]

11   "It Ain't Me Babe – A Struggle for Identity," *It Ain't Me Babe*, June 8, 1970, 11. Wagner Labor Archives, New York University.

12   Ellen Leo, "Power Trips," *It Ain't Me Babe*, September 17, 1970, 6. Wagner Labor Archives, New York University.

13   Alix Kates Shulman, "Emma Goldman's Feminism: A Reappraisal" in Shulman, ed., *Red Emma Speaks: An Emma Goldman Reader* (New York: Schocken Books, 1971), 4.

14   Shulman, "Emma Goldman's Feminism," 6.

15   Cathy Levine, "The Tyranny of Tyranny," *Black Rose* 1 (1974): 56. Anarchy Archives.

16   Emma Goldman Clinic, "Emma Goldman Clinic Mission Statement," http://www.emmagoldman.com/about/mission.html (accessed July 9, 2015).

17   "Emma Goldman," *Off Our Backs*, July 10, 1970, Wagner Labor Archives, New York University, 9; See also Candace Falk, *Love, Anarchy, and Emma Goldman* (New York: Holt, Rinehart, and Winston, 1984), and Kathy E. Ferguson, Emma Goldman *Political Thinking in the Streets* (Lanham: Rowman & Littlefield Publishers, 2011) for

discussions of Goldman's relationship with the feminist movement and working-class women's movement.

18   Chicago Anarcho-Feminists, "Who We Are: The Anarcho-Feminist Manifesto," *Siren* 1, no. 1 (April 1971). Anarchy Archives.

19   Ibid.

20   Arlene Meyers, "To Our Siren Subscribers," *Siren Journal*, No. 1. Weber, "On the Edge of All Dichotomies: Anarch@-Feminist Thought, Process and Action, 1970-1983.," 64.

21   "Black Cross Appears Again," *Siren Newsletter* 1, no. 3 (1972): 2.; Siren 1, no. 4 (1972): 8. Anarchy Archives.

22   Eden W, "The Other Side of the Coin," *Siren Newsletter*, no. 10 (1973). Anarchy Archives.

23   Ibid.

24   *How Sex Changed: A History of Transsexuality in the United States* (Cambridge, Mass.: Harvard University Press, 2004), 258.

25   Susan Stryker, *Transgender History* (Berkeley: Seal Press, 2008), 105.

26   Marie Leighton and Cathy Levine, "Blood of the Flower," *Siren*, no. 8 (1973), 5. Anarchy Archives.

27   Ibid.

28   Ibid.

29   Marie Leighton, "Letter," *Anarcha-Feminist Notes* 1, no. 2 (Spring 1977): 12. Anarchy Archives.

30   Elaine Leeder, "The Makings of An Anarchist Feminist," 1984, 2, Anarchy Archives.

31   Ibid.

32   Ibid.

33   Elaine Leeder, "Tiamat to Me," *Anarcho-Feminist Notes* 1, no. 2 (March 20, 1977), 14, Anarchy Archives.

34   *Siren Newsletter*, No. 2, and *Siren Journal*, No. 1. Slater, "Des Moines Women Form Support Group." Anarchy Archives.

35   Leeder, "Tiamat to Me."

36    Weber, "On the Edge of All Dichotomies," 103.

37    "Proposal to Merge the Anarcho-Feminist Network Notes and the Anarchist Feminist Communications Network," *Anarcho-Feminist Network Notes* 1, no. 3 (October 1975): 9. Anarchy Archives.

38    "Conference Flyer - Anarcha-Feminism: Growing Stronger" (TIAMAT Collective, June 9, 1978), Anarchy Archives.

39    Leeder, "The Makings of An Anarchist Feminist."

40    Conference Flyer - Anarcha-Feminism: Growing Stronger" (TIAMAT Collective, June 9, 1978), Anarchy Archives.

41    Barbara Ryan, *Feminism and the Women's Movement: Dynamics of Change in Social Movement Ideology*, and Activism (New York, NY: Psychology Press, 1992), 54.

42    Hellen Ellenbogen, "Feminism: The Anarchist Impulse Comes Alive," in *Emma's Daughters* (Unpublished, 1977), 6. Anarchy Archives.

43    Ibid., 5.

44    Evan Paxton, "Self Help Clinc Busted," Siren, 1972, 8 edition, Anarchy Archives. Also see Sandra Morgen, *Into Our Own Hands: The Women's Health Movement in the United States, 1969-1990* (New Brunswick, N.J: Rutgers University Press, 2002).

45    Farrow, "Feminism as Anarchism," 7. Also see Morgen, *Into Our Own Hands.*

46    Ellenbogen, "Feminism: The Anarchist Impulse Comes Alive," 7.

47    Ibid.

48    Kornegger, "Anarchism: The Feminist Connection."

49    Rebecca Staton, "Anarchism and Feminism," Anarcho-Feminist Network Notes 1, no. 3 (October 1975): 6. Anarchy Archives.

50    Judy Stein, *Anarchist Feminist Notes* 1, no. 1, 1976, 6 Anarchy Archives.

51    Come! Unity Press, "Some Thoughts On Money and Women's Culture," 1976, Anarchy Archives.

52    Peggy Kornegger, "Anarchism, Feminism, and Economics or: You Can't Have Your Pie and Share It Too," The Second Wave 4, no. 4 (Fall 1976): 4. Northeastern University Special Collections.

53    Ibid.

54    Mecca Reliance and Jean Horan, "Anarchist Conference April 19-21: Hunter College." Off Our Backs, May 31, 1974. Wagner Labor Archives, New York University.

55    Ibid.

56    Rosalyn Baxandall and Linda Gordon, *Dear Sisters: Dispatches From The Women's Liberation Movement* (New York, NY: Basic Books, 2001), 12.

57    Karen Johnson, "Mid West Conference," *Anarcho-Feminist Network Notes* 1, no. 3 (October 1975): 5. Anarchy Archives.

58    Marie Leighton, "Anarcho-Feminism and Louise Michel," Black Rose 1, no. 1 (1974): 14.

59    Karen Johnson, "Mid West Conference," *Anarcho-Feminist Network Notes* 1, no. 3 (October 1975): 5. Anarchy Archives.

60    Midge Slater, "Des Moines Women Form Support Group," *Anarchist Feminist Notes* 1, no. 1 (1976): 10. Anarchy Archives.

61    Grant Purdy, "Red Wing," *Anarcho-Feminist Notes* 1, no. 2 (Spring 1977): 7. Anarchy Archives.

62    Ibid. 8.

63    Marie Leighton, "Anarcho-Feminism and Louise Michel," *Black Rose* 1, no. 1 (1974): 8. Anarchy Archives.

64    Lizzie Borden, "Women and Anarchy," *Heresies* 1, no. 2 (1977): 74.

65    Ehrlich, "Socialism, Anarchism, and Feminism," 268.

66    Leighton, "Anarcho-Feminism and Louise Michel," 14.

67    Ehrlich, "Socialism, Anarchism, and Feminism," 26.

68    Patrick Murfin, "International Working Women's Day: Portrait of Penny Pixler,

Feminist and Wobbly," *The Industrial Worker*, March 8, 2015.

69    Ibid.

70    Ibid.

71    On the CWLU's split in 1976, see "The Chicago Women's Liberation Union: An Introduction," The Chicago Women's Liberation Union Herstory Website, 2000. Some members, angry at what they saw as the group's white middle class orientation unleashed a scathing attack on the organization's leadership at the 1976 International Women's Day event which denounced feminism, lesbianism and the ERA. The CWLU split over how to deal with this situation and officially disbanded in 1977. Penny Pixler, "Notes From China," *Whirlwind* 1, no. 11 (1978).

72    Carol Ehrlich, "Socialism, Anarchism, and Feminism," in *Reinventing Anarchy: What Are Anarchists Thinking These Days?*, ed. Howard Ehrlich (Routledge and Kegan Paul Books, 1977), 271.

73    "Situationists - an Introduction," Libcom.org, October 12, 2006 "Situationists - Reading Guide," Libcom.org

74    Ehrlich, "Socialism, Anarchism, and Feminism," 271.

75    Echols, *Daring To Be Bad*, 6.

76    Ibid., 252.

77    Ehrlich, "Socialism, Anarchism, and Feminism," 260.

78    Ibid.

79    Peggy Kornegger, "The Spirituality Ripoff," *The Second Wave* 4, no. 3 (Spring 1976): 18. Northeastern University Special Collections.

80    Ehrlich, "Socialism, Anarchism, and Feminism," 5.

81    Ibid.

82    Su Negrin, *Begin at Start* (Times Change Press, 1972), 128.; Kornegger, "Anarchism: The Feminist Connection."

83    Polletta, *Freedom Is an Endless Meeting*, 152.

84    Ibid., 160.

85    Baxandall and Gordon, Dear Sisters, 15.

86    Polletta, *Freedom Is an Endless Meeting*, 169.

87    Ibid., 152.

88    Ehrlich, "Socialism, Anarchism, and Feminism."

89    Ibid.

90    Jo Freeman, "The Tyranny of Structurelessness," *The Second Wave* 2, no. 1 (1972).

91    Ibid.

92    Ehrlich, "Socialism, Anarchism, and Feminism," 271.

93    Freeman, "The Tyranny of Structurelessness."

94    Ibid.

95    Cathy Levine, "The Tyranny of Tyranny" in *Untying the Knot: Feminism, Anarchism, and Organization* (Dark Star Press and Rebel Press, 1984).

96    Levine, "The Tyranny of Tyranny," 49.

97    Ibid., 53.

98    Ibid., 54.

99    Ehrlich, "Socialism, Anarchism, and Feminism," 271; Farrow, "Feminism as Anarchism."

100    Negrin, *Begin at Start*, 1.

101    Sue Katz, "An Anarchist Plebe Fights Back," *The Furies* 1, no. 4 (n.d.): 10.

102    Polletta, *Freedom Is an Endless Meeting*, 170.

103    Kornegger, "Anarchism: The Feminist Connection."

104    Barbara Epstein, *Political Protest and Cultural Revolution: Nonviolent Direct Action in the 1970s and 1980s* (Berkeley: University of California Press, 1991) 100.

105    Elaine Leeder, "Feminism as Anarchist Process," in *Quiet Rumours: An Anarcha-Feminist Reader*, ed. Dark Star Collective, 2nd edition (Edinburgh: AK Press, 2008).

106    Leeder, "The Makings of An Anarchist Feminist."

107    Weber, "On the Edge of All Dichotomies," 168.

108    Epstein, *Political Protest and Cultural Revolution*, 55.

109  Weber, "On the Edge of All Dichotomies,"133.

110  Leeder, "Feminism as Anarchist Process," 3.

111  Epstein, *Political Protest and Cultural Revolution*, 159.

112  Kytha Kurin, "Anarcha-Feminism: Why the Hyphen?" in *Only a Beginning: An Anarchist Anthology*, ed. Allan Antliff (Vancouver, BC.: Arsenal Pulp Press, 2004), 262.

113  Cindy Milstein, "'Occupy Anarchism': Musings on Prehistories, Present (Im)Perfects & Future (Im)Perfects," in *We Are Many: Reflections on Movement Strategy from Occupation to Liberation*, ed. Kate Khatib, Margaret Killjoy, and Mike McGuire, (Oakland: AK Press, 2012).

114  Kornegger, "Anarchism: The Feminist Connection," 248

115  Chris Dixon, *Another Politics: Talking Across Today's Transformative Movements* (Berkeley: University of California Press, 2014).

## ABOUT THE AUTHOR

*Julia Tanenbaum is a student in the Philadelphia area involved with United Students Against Sweatshops and environmental organizing. She studies history hoping to help build our movements today.*

# UNTIL ALL ARE FREE:
## BLACK FEMINISM, ANARCHISM, AND INTERLOCKING OPPRESSION

HILARY LAZAR

> If Black women were free, it would mean that everyone else would have to be free since our freedom would necessitate the destruction of all the systems of oppression.
>
> —The Combahee River Collective

> We are all feminists, united in our recognition that women's subordination exists. Our struggle needs to be fought alongside the struggle against other forms of oppression. We...are all anarchists, united in our belief for the need to create alternatives to this capitalist, patriarchal society wherein all are dominated and exploited.
>
> —Revolutionary Anarcha-Feminist Group of Dublin

There is growing recognition among activists that we need to acknowledge the interconnectedness of our struggles if we are to harness the collective power necessary to overcome interlocking systems of domination. As Francesca Mastrangelo comments in an editorial piece for *The Feminist Wire*, we need to begin to "recognize that our liberation is bound up in the liberation of every person."[1] Or, as expressed by labor organizer Ai-Jen Poo, "The way we try to think about it and the way the world is, we're all interdependent and interconnected... Those connections are fairly invisible to most people most of the time. We're taught not to see those connections."[2] In part, this sentiment—the need

Art by Melanie Cervantes | justseeds.org

to recognize that "we" are an "us"—may speak to the times. Since the heyday of the alter-globalization movement in the late 1990s and early 2000s, critiques of global capitalism and neoliberalism have been a thread across mobilizations. This current has only become more pronounced in the wake of the financial crisis of 2008–2009 and the widespread adoption of austerity measures that benefited big business, banks, and those in power, at the expense of everyone else. And economic inequality and the trend towards corporatization only continue to deepen. Consequently, it comes as no surprise that there is a sense of common cause across struggles in their shared anticapitalist thrust.

There is also an atmosphere of intense urgency in recent movements, as we seem to have reached a crisis point on numerous fronts. The deleterious impact of climate change is ever more evident as extreme weather disasters are becoming par for the course. Fascism appears to be rearing its ugly head in Europe, and now here in the US with Trump's surge in popularity. And people of color and trans* folks face daily instances of systemic oppression, the possibility of violence and death or other threats. So, feelings that "we're all in this together" and the need to find ways to cooperate, at the risk of financial, climatic, and societal collapse, may also be contributing to calls for united struggle.

Yet, along with the current historical moment, there may be another reason activists are coming to see their efforts as intertwined—namely, the importance of Black feminism in contemporary activist thought. In fact, while Jo Reger has noted that feminism is everywhere and has "become a part of everyday cultural beliefs and norms," and "like fluoride...is simply in the water," it is equally arguable that Black feminism in particular has come to inform current activist culture in the way it underscores interlocking oppressions.[3]

It also seems that the analysis of Black feminism has a particularly deep resonance with anarchist understandings of mechanisms of power, which similarly foreground a linking across all systems of domination. Again, this is important to note, so as to ensure that the impact of Black feminism on contemporary anarchism is not overlooked. This currency across the two schools of thought is also notable, however, as it very well may be the coming together of Black feminism and anarchism that is encouraging the shift in orientation away from a more fragmented conceptualization of struggle, and towards the idea of our struggles as interdependent. And, especially given the increased presence of anarchism in mobilizations since the Zapatista uprising in 1994, it seems plausible that the confluence of these streams of thought is having a powerful combined impact on radical political thought and culture.

Regardless of what is driving it, the notion of interlocking oppressions holds real revolutionary potential. In underscoring the connectedness of all forms of domination, it leads to creation of stronger movements that are capable of mounting more successful challenges to oppressive systems by breaking down structural barriers that prevent communities from building power. However, the question remains as to how activists can begin to move beyond simply espousing their connectedness towards actual practices of working to address domination simultaneously in all its forms. Looking to Black feminism and anarchism can help to advance theoretical and practical models for how to do so.

## BLACK FEMINISM: FROM INTERSECTIONALITY TO INTERLOCKING OPPRESSIONS

As Karma Chavéz and Cindy Griffin comment in the introduction to their collection of essays on intersections in communication scholarship, "During the midst of multiple, interwoven struggles for liberation catalyzed in the middle of the twentieth century, in the United States, feminists of color, working-class feminists, and lesbians articulated the 'interlocking' nature, as well as the 'double' or 'multiple jeopardy' of having several oppressed identities."[4] One of the earliest and most influential articulations of this was Black feminist legal scholar Kimberlé Crenshaw's concept of "intersectionality." There have been, however, numerous expressions of what metaphor or concept best illustrates the complex nature of multiple oppressions. Among these, the idea of interlocking oppressions as posed by the Combahee River Collective perhaps best captures the interconnectedness of all systems of domination.

In 1989, Crenshaw first debuted the idea of "intersectionality" in her essay, "Demarginalizing the Intersection of Race and Sex." Noting that "the experiences of women of color, poor, and immigrant women are subsumed and erased in legal practices, political decisions, and social norms," Crenshaw explains that this erasure reflects an inability to "think outside of singular axes of identity" and results in the assumption that all women are middle-class white women.[5] To illustrate this, she suggests that domination should instead be thought of as analogous to a four-way traffic intersection in which injury can come from a number of directions: "[It] may flow in one direction, and it may flow in another. If an accident happens in an intersection, it can be caused by cars traveling from any number of directions and, sometimes, from all of them. Similarly, if a Black woman is harmed because she is in an intersection, her injury could result from sex discrimination or race discrimination."[6] While clearly a critical and necessary intervention into Second Wave feminist thought and the invisibility of interactions across racial, class, sexual and gender analysis, too often this particular metaphor has been limited by its interpretation of oppression as having an "additive" quality, rather than a more slippery and dynamic relationship.

Consequently, feminist theorists have struggled to find alternative ways to best capture the messiness and conceptual complexity of the overlapping, interactive nature of multiple oppressions. Adding nuance to Crenshaw's notion of intersectionality, these theories have sought to underscore the ways in which multifaceted identities are shaped by the many structures of domination and ever-shifting contexts. These metaphors have included everything from Cherríe Moraga and Gloria Anzaldúa's "Theory in the Flesh" to María Lugones' "Curdling." And as Chavéz and Griffin comment, "Each metaphor or perspective offer[s] something slightly different."[7] Yet, the idea of "interlocking" oppressions seems to be most instructive for understanding the ways in which, regardless of the exact relational nature between the specific sets of oppressions in any given case, one thing remains certain—that all forms of subjugation and domination are integrally related to one another, and that striving for an end of any form of oppression necessitates struggling to end all oppressions. They are not only intersecting, but are inextricably tied together.

This conceptualization of interlocking oppressions was first expressed by the Combahee River Collective more than a decade prior to Crenshaw's coining of the term "intersectionality." Writing in 1977, this group of Black feminist lesbians issued a statement in which they asserted that

> the most general statement of our politics at the present time would be that we are actively committed to struggling against racial, sexual, heterosexual, and class oppression, and see as our particular task the development of integrated analysis and practice based upon the fact that the major systems of oppression are interlocking. The synthesis of these oppressions creates the conditions of our lives. As Black women we see Black feminism as the logical political movement to combat the manifold and simultaneous oppressions that all women of color face.[8]

As they argue, it would be impossible to address only a single issue at a time. In other words, as Black women, as Black women lesbians, as Black women lesbian workers, as Black women lesbian workers with family, and from communities where others remained subjugated for numerous

reasons—in order to be truly liberated requires addressing these simultaneou occurring and inseparable experiences of oppression. Hence, their insistence that "...we are not just trying to fight oppression on one front or even two, but instead to address a whole range of oppressions...if Black women were free it would mean that everyone else would have to be free since our freedom would necessitate the destruction of all the systems of oppression."[9]

Or as they write elsewhere in the statement, "We believe that sexual politics under patriarchy is as pervasive in Black women's lives as are the politics of class and race. We also often find it difficult to separate race from class from sex oppression because in our lives they are most often experienced simultaneously."[10] Consequently, they maintain that one cannot even conceptually parse them out and must instead conceive the idea of "racial-sexual oppression." Moreover, although it was a "combined anti-racist and anti-sexist position [that] drew [them] together initially," over time, the Collective members had come to realize that, along with addressing heterosexism, "the liberation of all oppressed peoples necessitates the destruction of the political-economic systems of capitalism and imperialism as well as patriarchy."[11] In other words, in order to contest any form of subjugation means the need to take on "the System" as a whole.

To be sure, other analytical frameworks certainly offer useful theoretical contributions to unpacking the dynamic, overlapping, and interactive nature of oppression. Yet this more holistic understanding put forth by the Combahee River Collective on the interrelated and interlocking dimensions to systems of domination is essential for understanding how power, privilege, and subjugation operate in contemporary society. Given what can be considered the deeply diffused Foucauldian capillaries of power throughout society, coupled with the overarching reach of capitalism and corresponding systems of racial-sexual domination into every facet of life, it would be impossible to address each instance of oppression a single case at a time.

By extension, if all oppression needs to be confronted concurrently, the Combahee idea of interlocking oppression is also vital, as it suggests a need for a politics of solidarity. For instance, although they recognize the complicity of Black men in upholding patriarchy, they also recognize the subjugation of Black men along lines of race and/or class. Similarly, while white feminists very actively participated in upholding racism, they were nonetheless impacted by patriarchal domination. In other words, context is key for understanding the complicated and dynamic nature of domination and subjugation. Oppressors may be oppressed, and oppressed may be oppressors—so the only solution is to work together to eliminate all forms of oppression.

Since the Combahee first issued their Statement, Black feminists and other activists have taken on this language of interlocking oppression. For example, Black feminist and lesbian poet Audre Lorde, in her 1985 address, "I am Your Sister: Black Women Organizing Across Sexualities," draws directly on this approach to oppression theory. In this talk she speaks to the prevalence of homophobia in Black feminism and Black women's activism,

commenting, "When I say I am a Black feminist, I mean I recognize that my power as well as my primary oppressions come as a result of my Blackness as well as my womanness, and therefore my struggle on both these fronts are inseparable."[12] Along with these inseparable struggles, she also calls on her audience to recognize the necessity of contesting homophobia with these efforts as well. As she comments, "Homophobia . . . is a waste of woman energy, and it puts a terrible weapon into the hands of your enemies to be used against you to silence you, to keep you docile and in line. It also serves to keep us isolated and apart."[13]

This kind of exclusion, she explains, does a disservice to the movement as it robs it of the "vital insights and energies" of Black women who are part of the wider "Black family," regardless of their sexuality.[14] In essence, by failing to see their struggles as related, and by actively excluding Black lesbians from Black feminist spaces, they were limiting their radical potentiality to overturn patriarchy, while bolstering heteronormativity. For this same reason, she demands recognition for the interconnectedness—and the possibility of this interconnectedness—of being a Black, a woman, and a lesbian, insisting that these oppressions can and do exist simultaneously, hence demanding simultaneous "destruction" (to draw on the language of the Combahee River Collective).

Patricia Hill Collins also underscores interlocking notions of oppression in her concept of the "matrix of domination."[15] As she explains, "Black feminist thought fosters a fundamental paradigmatic shift in how we think about oppression. By embracing a paradigm of race, class, and gender as interlocking systems of oppression, Black feminist thought re-conceptualizes the social relations of domination and resistance."[16] Collins, however, explicitly emphasizes the importance of avoiding "additive models" for understanding dynamics of oppression reflected "in the either/or dichotomous thinking of Eurocentric, masculinist thought."[17] This, she argues, fails to capture the dynamic and multiple axes and levels of oppression, hence necessitating adoption of a "both/and" model.

bell hooks, in her idea of a "politics of domination," further helps to elucidate this paradigm shift. As she explains, looking at the multiple axes of oppression such as race, class, and gender and their situational relationships elucidates the ways in which they share "ideological ground." This common ground is "a belief in domination, and a belief in the notions of superior and inferior, which are components of all of those systems...[It]'s like a house, they share the foundation, but the foundation is the ideological beliefs around which notions of domination are constructed."[19]

In a very similar way, over a decade later, in "White Privilege and Male Privilege: A Personal Account of Coming to See Correspondences Through Work in Women's Studies," Peggy McIntosh speaks about the interlocking nature of oppression. In this piece, McIntosh discusses the invisibility of systems of privilege that confer unearned benefits and resources on certain social groups at the expense of others— namely, men at the expense of women, and whites at the expense of people of color, or heteronormative individuals at the expense of homosexual and gender

non-conforming persons. In so doing, however, she seeks to avoid the pitfall of an additive approach to understanding oppression. As she comments,

One factor seems clear about all of the interlocking oppressions. They take both active forms that we can see and embedded forms that members of the dominant group are taught not to see. In my class and place, I did not see myself as racist because I was taught to recognize racism only in individual acts of meanness by members of my group, never in invisible systems conferring racial dominance on my group from birth. Likewise, we are taught to think that sexism or heterosexism is carried on only through intentional, individual acts of discrimination, meanness, or cruelty, rather than in invisible systems conferring unsought dominance on certain groups.[20]

To be fair, there are certainly significant limitations in the theoretical usefulness of privilege theory, and an identity politics corresponding with this. Namely, much like additive approaches to intersectionality, privilege theory can be grossly reductionist, erasing more complex relational dynamics of power and oppression. And we might easily critique McIntosh for failing to actually incorporate an interlocking model of oppression in her analysis of privilege. Even so, the salient point here is that McIntosh's piece is clear evidence of the infusion of Black feminist discourse into generalized understandings of oppression and domination among white feminists. In fact, this piece in particular may have had an especially influential role in helping the broader diffusion of Black feminism into activist theories of power, as it remains one of the foundational essays (for better or worse) used in activist anti-oppression trainings. So, again, although McIntosh may not have ultimately avoided relying on an additive theoretical model, it is still noteworthy that she also explicitly states that these mechanisms of domination are interlocking.

## ANARCHISM: COLLECTIVE SELF-LIBERATION FOR ALL

Although a bit of a question of the chicken and the egg, we can see a similar adoption of this type of interlocking analysis of oppression in contemporary anarchism. To be sure, conceptualization of systems of control as interconnected, and hence requiring the concurrent rooting out of all forms of domination, is at the very heart of anarchist theory and praxis. That being said, contemporary anarchist thought also undoubtedly reflects the influence of Black feminists such as Audre Lorde, James Baldwin, and bell hooks among countless other Third and Fourth Wave scholars. Indeed, this is particularly evident in queer anarchism and poststructuralist anarcha-feminisms. Either way, there is at the very least a clear resonance across the two. And given the prominent role anarchism has played in twenty-first-century movements—what some suggest has been an "anarchist turn" in activism—it becomes all the more necessary to consider the connections across them.[21]

In order to understand the relationship between anarchism and its emphasis on interlocking oppressions, it is helpful to look at its historical roots and philosophical underpinnings.

Contemporary or traditional Western anarchism—what is considered to be "classical" anarchism—has always been predicated on the belief that one must look at all centralization of power as problematic, and view all systems of domination as inextricably interrelated.[22] Seeking to make sense of the rapidly changed social landscape in the wake of industrialization, nineteenth-century anarchist thinkers such as Mikhail Bakunin, Pierre-Joseph Proudhon and Max Stirner, among others, endeavored to resolve how to respond to new forms of inequality and coercion that now derived less from feudal or manorial rule than from an increasingly centralized state and exploitative labor conditions under capitalism. Unlike their Marxist counterparts, however, for whom the primary concern was the working class, for these early anarchists the real goal was to ensure freedom from domination of all types and for all peoples—including women and men, and (usually) people of all races. As Bakunin expresses,

What all other men are is of the greatest importance to me. However independent I may imagine myself to be, however far removed I may appear from mundane considerations by my social status, I am enslaved to the misery of the meanest member of society. The outcast is my daily menace. Whether I am Pope, Czar, Emperor, or even Prime Minister, I am always the creature of their circumstance, the conscious product of their ignorance, want and clamoring. They are in slavery, and I, the superior one, am enslaved in consequence.[23]

This emphasis on the necessity of eliminating all forms of oppression as integral to attaining a fully free society has remained one of the fundamental principles of anarchist thought. To be sure, being anti-doctrinaire, anarchists may conceive of numerous visions and versions for what this may look like in practice, or what steps are necessary for achieving this form of liberated society. As Peter Marshall describes, anarchism is "a broad river" within which "it is possible to discern a number of distinct currents."[24] In the most general of terms, however, some of the primary concerns for anarchists are with ensuring freedom for all from domination and top-down coercion of any kind, and the ability for all humans (and living beings, for that matter) to achieve their highest potential and the greatest well-being possible. Moreover, this further implies that all are freely able to participate in the decisions that shape their lives, while enjoying equal access to the resources necessary to do so.

Necessarily, this idea of a free society as being dependent on whether or not all members are liberated implies that one cannot decouple one's own liberation from that of another. Alexander Berkman summarizes this nicely in "ABC of Anarchism":

Anarchism means that you should be free; that no one should enslave you, boss you, rob you, or impose upon you. It means that you should be free to do the things you want to do; and that you should not be compelled to do what you don't want to do. It means that you should have a chance to choose the kind of a life you want to live, and live it without anybody interfering.

It means that the next fellow should have the same freedom as you, that every one should have the same rights and liberties. It means that all men are brothers, and that they should live like brothers, in peace and harmony. That is to say, that there should be no war, no violence used by one set of men against another, no monopoly and no poverty, no oppression, no taking advantage of your fellow-man. In short, Anarchism means a condition or society where all men and women are free, and where all enjoy equally the benefits of an ordered and sensible life.[25]

Simply looking at these principles, it is easy enough to see the resonance with the Combahee collective's perspective on interrelated struggle. There is the idea of one's personal liberation being dependent on the liberation of all. There is emphasis on empathetic concern for the well-being of others, not out of obligation or paternalist duty, but rather from the notion of a shared struggle and shared fate among all living beings. And there are the ways in which this perception catalyzes reciprocity, cooperation, and mutual aid—other mainstays in both Black feminist and anarchist practice.

Certainly, there is also a long tradition of feminist-informed anarchist thought dating back to the late-eighteenth century, which helped to clarify understandings of the interdependence of struggles with a feminist lens. As explained by Roxanne Dunbar-Ortiz in the introduction to *Quiet Rumors*, a collection of anarcha-feminist texts, "Up until recently the terms anarchism and feminism were rarely found in the same sentence, much less interpreted as integrally related, Emma Goldman being the single example people could identify."[26] Yet, as she points out, there were countless others lost to the annals of history—Lucy Parsons, Mother Jones, Helen Keller, Louise Michel and "thousands of other historical figures and contemporary feminist anarchists."[27] These women were helping to advance the critical perspective that "true equality can never be achieved within the capitalist system . . . [and] we need to be clear that when feminist gains are won, it is in the name of true equality for all people . . . [r]eal feminism requires complete social restructuring which can essentially be equated with true anarchism."[28]

Even in the early days, there were some threads within anarchism coming from feminists of color who helped to further push anarchist political theory towards even more recognition of the dynamic, overlapping nature of all oppressions. Lucy Parsons—one of the founders of the Industrial Workers of the World and widow of Haymarket martyr Albert Parsons—was one of the first celebrated anarchists of color, having likely been born a slave and documented as having both Mexican and Native American ancestry. Reflecting her commitment to syndicalism, she provided incisive critique of divided struggles and called on radicals to "sink such differences as nationality, religion, politics, and set our eyes eternally and forever toward the rising star of the industrial republic of labor."[29] Meanwhile, in Argentina, early anarcha-feminists, some of whom helped to publish *La Voz de La Mujer*, saw their "anarchist feminist propaganda . . . [a]s inseparable from a growing awareness of the mechanisms of economic and social exploitation of

Argentinean women with immigrant origins," and as "[materializing] these working women's expectations within a vast project for a libertarian society."[30]

Yet it is in contemporary forms of anarcha-feminism that we see explicit connection with (and influence of) Black feminism in terms of emphasizing simultaneity of struggle. In "Insurrection at the Intersections: Feminism, Intersectionality, and Anarchism," Jen Rogue and Abbey Volcano put anarchism in conversation with Black feminism and offer a specifically anarchist critique of the "additive" approach to intersectionality. Instead, they highlight the importance of adopting a lens "through which to view race, class, gender, sexuality, etc. as mutually-constituting processes . . . categories [that] do not exist independently from one another; [but] rather, they mutually reinforce one another . . . [in] overlapping, complex, interacting, intersecting, and often contradictory" ways.[31]

Meanwhile Chris Crass, founder of the Catalyst Project, directly speaks to how Black feminism informed "the anarchism taken up and developed in the 1990s [which] was a product of the movement experiences of the preceding four decades," including "The Black Freedom movement, the women's liberation movement, and other liberation movements . . . challenging multiple forms of oppression."[32] In fact, he credits the Combahee River Collective's "'integrated analysis of oppression" that "suggests that systems of racism, capitalism, heteropatriarchy, and ableism operate with and through each other . . . interconnected" as "truly revolutionary" and highly influential for the anarchists of the 1990s who "increasingly took up this 'integrated analysis.'"[33] In an interview, Crass further explains how, for the Catalyst Project, intersectionality specifically means taking on a more "collective" approach to liberatory politics by

> ... addressing our privilege as white people by examining the differences in the ways those privileges manifest based on gender, class, sexual orientation, ability, etc. Intersectionality complicates how we understand relationships of power and what's needed to transform them ... If intersectionality is a framework for recognizing the ways in which oppressions are wrapped up together and structure society, then collective liberation is a corresponding framework for looking at how we organize to transform those relations of power. [It] is an approach to organizing that recognizes that our liberation as white people is wrapped up with and dependent on the liberation of communities of color who are living on the front lines of racial and economic oppression.[34]

Similarly, Richard Day, in his account on anarchist currents within contemporary movements, describes how "feminist critiques of power" have come to be a critical influence on alter-globalization organizing.[35] Moreover, as he sees it, due to their increasing anarchist underpinnings, there is a growing confluence across struggles as they come to adopt what he refers to as a "groundless solidarity/infinite responsibility"—the idea that "increasing numbers of people all over the world are converging on the notion that the new global order needs to be fought on all levels, in all localities, through multiple, disparate—interlocking—struggles."[36]

Chris Dixon's recent work, *Another Politics: Talking Across Today's Transformative Movements*, however, perhaps most expressly addresses the relationship between anarchism and Black feminism, as well as interlocking oppressions, as he specifically focuses his analysis of contemporary movements on the interconnectedness of struggle.[37] Dixon reflects on the ways that contemporary movement participants—from indigenous rights to labor to racial justice mobilizations—have come to understand their struggles as shared. As he notes, for these activists, it is clear that

> systems of oppression and exploitation—whether we're talking about patriarchy, heterosexism, white supremacy, ableism, capitalism, so on—actually work with and through one another and cannot be disentangled from one another. And in fact require, if we're going to try and ultimately do away with them and create a different way of relating, a whole different social structure. That's going to require us to have a kind of multilayered revolutionary politics that takes on all of these things at once.[38]

In particular, Dixon highlights the coming together of three political currents—Black feminism, prison abolitionism, and anarchism—as formative for the kind of "integrated analysis" and antiauthoritarian sentiment that he argues has come to be at the heart of contemporary activism in the US and Canada.

## TOWARDS A UNITED STRUGGLE

What, then, is the importance of recognizing a perception of interrelatedness of struggles among activists and the relationship between Black feminism and anarchism? To begin with, at the very least it suggests a need to acknowledge the critical value of Black feminist thought in contemporary activism. To date there remains a deeply problematic erasure of the important contributions by activists of color and feminist scholars of color from our movement theory and literature. This not only replicates racist-sexist dynamics of power in how we talk about and understand our struggles, but in our interpersonal relationships and internal movement dynamics as well. It also points to a natural resonance across Black (and Third/Fourth wave) feminism and anarchism—which has been largely overlooked by activists and academics alike. These facts alone suggest a reason to explore activist conceptualizations of interlocking oppressions.

At a practical level, there are still other reasons for considering the interconnectedness of struggles and the salience of the relationship between anarchism and Black feminism. To begin with, at a more emotive or affective level, this implies a changed subjectivity, wherein we are beginning to see ourselves as intimately connected with others outside our own individualized lives or direct experiences. There is a transcendence of divisions—a sense of coming together, common cause, and shared humanity. This sense of "relatedness" among activists also points to the potential for deeper engagement in politics of solidarity. Indeed, interlocking oppression theory as articulated by both anarchism and Black feminism is instructive for moving beyond the rhetoric of interconnected struggle to real actionable solidarity, in providing specific models for how activists can rethink working together.

For instance, the Bay Area Fireworks Collective's *Revolutionary Solidarity: A Critical Reader for Accomplices* offers a powerful and important critique of the concept of "allyship." The pieces in the reader suggest that the term "ally" has become bound up with liberal identity politics and "the ally industrial complex," and ultimately been "rendered meaningless." For this reason, the authors recommend adoption of the term "accomplice" as a way to shift towards a more interlocking approach to understanding struggles, and as a way to emphasize action over words.

As one essay comments, while being an ally has come to be adopted by white activists seeking recognition as antiracist and paying lip service to their commitment to racial justice, being an accomplice moves past superficial or patronizing forms of false solidarity. Rather, it means acknowledging that as long as any are oppressed, then all are subjected to the mutually-reinforcing systems of domination. They suggest that

. . .[this] framework of solidarity affirms that other groups have something of worth to be gained through interactions with them, whether materially or by gaining something less tangible like perspective, joy, or inspiration. The solidarity model also dispels the idea of one inside and one outside, foregrounding how individuals belong to multiple groups and groups overlap with one another, while demanding respect for the identity and self-sufficiency of each of those groups.[39]

Allied frameworks, however, underscore "ideas of I and the other" as opposed to a more united, collective conceptualization.[40] Moreover, the accomplice model reinforces the notion that struggles are inextricably bound together. As explained in "Accomplices Not Allies: Abolishing the Ally Industrial Complex,"

> The risks of an ally who provides support or solidarity (usually on a temporary basis) in a fight are much different than that of an accomplice. When we fight back or forward, together, becoming complicit in a struggle toward liberation, we are accomplices.[41]

Along with the anarchist emphasis on shifting from an allied politics to the solidarity politics of being accomplices, another possible inroad for promoting a more interlocking feminism within activist spaces is in the idea that that one learns by doing—something that Third Wave, Chicana-feminist scholar Aimee Carrillo Rowe's "politics of relation" illuminates. In her article, "Be Long: Toward a Feminist Politics of Relation," Rowe argues that whom we love is political. As she comments, "The sites of our belonging constitute how we see the world, what we value, who we are (becoming)."[42] Consequently, she aims to "make transparent" the political conditions that shape our belonging and affective ties. Ultimately, she suggests that in order for us to be able to struggle together we need to develop "coalitional subjectivities" that arise through working together across difference while adopting a "politics of relation." This occurs through the very act of doing together, when individuals jump into alliances allowing us "to see [our] oppression and privilege as inextricably bound to others and [in which we] cannot envision [our] existence and politics as separate from others' existence and politics."[43] In turn, this enables activists to build a politics across power lines, so that they can begin to understand their respective experiences and collaborate towards an emancipatory struggle for all.

Certainly this may be easier said then done; yet Rowe's call for us to reject normative relations predicated on "power over" in favor of "power with," which means a turning "towards" one another, is another example of the kind of shift necessary for advancing a stronger movement for the liberation of all.[44] As she writes, what we most need is to see "that radical modes of belonging hold tremendous potential for transforming who we think we are and how we imagine something called 'feminism.' This is the aim of a politics of relation . . . the inclination of one toward another, as the basis for community, intimacy, and awareness."[45] In sum, then, as Rowe suggests, perhaps the best way to encourage the development of an interlocking feminist framework is in fact to begin to relate to one another through our interlocked positions. It is not only our oppressions and privileges that are inseparably intertwined, but we ourselves. Recognizing this kinship within our individual experiences or put more simply, our shared humanity—together with the anarchist call for the critical need to work together as accomplices and not allies—may be the best route to our collective liberation.

Still, there continues to be an absence of nuanced analysis of what it means to adopt an interlocking framework in practice. For many, this leads to a naïve and deeply problematic erasure of difference in favor of a totalizing universal understanding of how oppression operates. Calls for empathetic recognition of common cause can lead to the pitfall of reinscribing oppressive dynamics and eliminating differences of experience. This is something that anarcha-feminists such as Rogue and Volcano speak to directly—making the relevance of examining anarchism hand in hand with intersectional and interlocking analysis all the more clear. As they note, "We call for an end to all exploitation and oppression," yet they further observe the necessity of avoiding reducing or flattening "all these social relations into a single framework" in a way that fails to account for how "the gamut of hierarchically-arranged social relations are in their own ways unique."[46] Or, as they further explain,

As anarchists, we have found that intersectionality is useful to the degree that it can inform our struggles. Intersectionality has been helpful for understanding the ways that oppressions overlap and play out in people's everyday lives. However, when interpreted through liberal frameworks, typical intersectional analyses often assume myriad oppressions to function identically, which can preclude class analysis, an analysis of the state, and analyses of ruling institutions. Our assessment is that everyday experiences of oppressions and exploitation are important and useful for struggle if we utilize intersectionality in a way that can encompass the different methods through which white supremacy, heteronormativity,

patriarchy, class society etc. function in people's lives, rather than simply listing them as though they all operate in similar fashions.[47]

Chris Crass makes a similar point about his organization's antiracist work, and admits that "we've made a mistake about applying intersectionality to our work; in some cases we organized white people as if they were a homogenous group . . . and we've alienated people we were working with by flattening out differences that can actually be a source of power."[48] In short then, as these writers suggest, adopting an interlocking framework requires recognizing the uniqueness of differences—"unity in diversity," to use a term favored by social ecologist and libertarian communalist, Murray Bookchin—or of the divergent systems of social domination, and each individual experience of subjugation, as being central to a nuanced analysis of mechanisms of control. If all forms of subjugation are reduced to a single axis, oppression cannot be contested, and indeed may only be reified. Consequently, anarchist and Black feminist approaches to interlocking analysis help to underscore this need to account for complexity, uniqueness, and dynamism within the mechanisms of power.

Even so, it is one thing to say that we need to take a cue from Black feminism and anarchism in adopting an approach to oppression analysis that recognizes difference, and another to understand how to navigate the challenges of doing so in actual practices of solidarity. How does one account for difference of experience, or the fact that society confers power on some at the expense of others, while still working towards the simultaneous collective liberation of all? One need only think of the profoundly problematic calls being made by some alleged "allies" to adopt the motto of #AllLivesMatter to see a clear example of how an ostensibly interlocking approach—"we all matter and need liberating, right?"—can still lead to oppression.

One possible solution may be to turn to a new metaphor for interlocking oppression—that of a tangled knot. There are countless strands in this knot, each one representing a different expression of domination, and all tightly bound together. Given their entanglement, it is therefore necessary to loosen all the strands if the knot is to be undone. In some moments, however, one strand may need more immediate attention and loosening than others. In other moments, perhaps it may be necessary to pull on multiple strands at once. While the knot of oppression will remain ensnared until all strands are freed, it is vital to understand that interdependent as the threads may be, each must be attended to both as an individual strand and as part of the collective tangle. This kind of conceptualization helps to avoid totalizing "alls" that erase distinct experiences of subjugation, while still allowing for an understanding that "none are free until all are free." In any case, as we endeavor to figure out how to put into practice a better politics of solidarity based on an understanding of shared and interdependent struggle, at least we have both Black feminism and anarchism as theoretical and practical models to help point us in the right direction.

## NOTES

1    Francesca Mastrangelo, "Love Is Not Enough: A Response to the Love as a Radical Act Forum." *FeministWire*, October 29, 2013.

2    Sally Kohn, "Activists Use Love and Empathy to Create New Alliances and Possibilities with the 'Enemy,'" *YES! Magazine*, July 1, 2013.

3    Jo Reger, *Everywhere and Nowhere: Contemporary Feminism in the United States* (New York: Oxford University Press, 2012), 5.

4    Karma Chávez and Cindy Griffin, *Standing in the Intersection: Feminist Voices, Feminist Practices in Communication Studies* (Albany: SUNY Press, 2012), 5.

5    Chávez and Griffin, *Standing in the Intersection*, 4.

6    Kimberlé Williams Crenshaw, "Mapping the Margins: Intersectionality, Identity Politics, and Violence Against Women of Color," *Stanford Law Review* 43 (1991), 1241-1299.

7    Chávez and Griffin, *Standing in the Intersection*, 4

8    Combahee River Collective, "A Black Feminist Statement, 1977," in Cherríe Moraga and Gloria Anzaldúa, eds., *This Bridge Called My Back: Writings by Radical Women of Color* (New York: Kitchen Table / Women of Color Press, 1983), 210.

9    Combahee River Collective, "A Black Feminist Statement, 1977," 215.

10    Ibid, 213.

11    Ibid

12    Audre Lorde, "I Am Your Sister: Black Women Organizing Across Sexualities," (Women of Color/Kitchen Table Press, 1985), 3.

13    Ibid, 6.

14    Ibid, 7.

15    Patricia Hill Collins, "Black Feminist Thought in the Matrix of Domination" in *Black Feminist Thought: Knowledge, Consciousness, and the Politics of Empowerment* (Boston: Unwin Hyman, 1990). 221–238

16    Ibid.

17    Ibid.

18    Ibid.

19    Ibid.

20    Peggy McIntosh, "White Privilege and Male Privilege: A Personal Account of Coming to See Correspondences Through Work in Women's Studies," *Working Paper No. 189*. (Wellesley Coll., Mass. Center for Research on Women, 1986).

21    Duane Rouselle and Süreyyya Evren, eds., *The Anarchist Turn Symposium*, May 2011.

22    It is important to make the distinction here that what I am looking at, and what is typically considered classical anarchism and of the anarchist canon is largely Western in origin, beginning in mid-eighteenth-century Europe (albeit, including Russia, which is also part of Asia). That said, there is arguably a much longer and deeper tradition of anarchist thought (or, if not in name, at least anarchist sensibility) that extends back as far as many of the ancient Eastern philosophies and certainly beyond the boundaries of the West. For an important collection on non-Western anarchism see Raymond Craib and Barry Maxwell eds., *No Gods, No Masters, No Peripheries: Global Anarchisms* (Oakland: PM Press, 2015) as well as Maia Ramnath's *Decolonizing Anarchism: An Antiauthoritarian History of India's Liberation Struggle* (Oakland: IAS/AK Press, 2011).

23    Mikhail Bakunin, "Solidarity in Liberty: The Workers' Path to Freedom," 1867.

24    Peter Marshall, *Demanding the Impossible: A History of Anarchism* (Oakland: PM Press, 2009), 6.

25    Alexander Berkman, *ABC of Anarchism* (Freedom Press: 1977, reprint 1929.

26    Roxanne Dunbar-Ortiz. "Quiet Rumors: An Introduction" in Dark Star Collective, *Quiet Rumors: An Anarcha-Feminist Reader*, Third Ed., (Oakland: AK Press, 2012), 11.

27    Ibid.

28    Revolutionary Anarcha-Feminist Group, "Why Anarcha-Feminism?" in *Quiet Rumors* (2012), 14.

29    Lucy Parsons. "1905 Speech to the IWW."

30    H. Finet, "Female Anarchism and Conviviality Among Workpeople in Buenos Aires (1890-1920)," in Gwendolyn Windpassinger, *Queer Anarcha-feminism: An Emerging Ideology? The Case of Proyectil Fetal*, Diss. 2012,138.

31    Jen Rogue and Abbey Volcano, "Insurrection at the Intersection" in *Quiet Rumors* (2012), 48.

32    Chris Crass, *Towards Collective Liberation: Anti-Racist Organizing, Feminist Praxis, and Movement Building Strategy* (Oakland: PM Press, 2013), 3. The Catalyst Project is an activist training organization that focuses on racial justice and workers' rights.

33    Ibid, 5.

34    Ibid, 255. Here Crass is directly referencing the Combahee conceptualization of interlocking oppressions.

35    Richard Day, *Gramsci is Dead: Anarchist Currents in the Newest Social Movements* (Ann Arbor, MI; Pluto Press, 2005),197.

36    Ibid, 201-2.

37    Chris Dixon, *Another Politics: Talking Across Today's Transformative Movements* (Berkeley: University of California Press, 2015).

38    Carwil Bjork-James, "Beyond a Radical Minority: An Interview with Anarchist Writer Chris Dixon," 2015.

39    Anon, "A Critique of Ally Politics" in Fireworks Collective and Cindy Milstein eds., *Revolutionary Solidarity: A Critical*

*Reader for Accomplices*, 2015, 6.

40      Ibid, 6.

41      Occupy Oakland. "Accomplices Not Allies: Abolishing the Ally Industrial Complex" in *Revolutionary Solidarity*, 2014), 35.

42      Aimee Carrillo Rowe, "Be Longing: Toward a Feminist Politics of Relation," NWSA Journal, 17 (2005),16.

43      Chávez and Griffin, *Standing in the Intersection*, 11.

44      Rowe, "Be Longing," 37.

45      Ibid, 45.

46      Rogue and Volcano, "Insurrection at the Intersection," 44.

47      Ibid, 45.

48      Crass, Towards Collective Liberation, 255.

## ABOUT THE AUTHOR

*Hillary is a past recipient of an IAS writing grant.*

*Hillary Lazar has been involved with anarchist, radical education, and social justice projects since the 90s. She is a doctoral student and instructor of Sociology and is currently focused on efforts to organize graduate students. She is a cofounder of the University of Pittsburgh's Student Anarchist Graduate Association, a collective member of the Big Idea Bookstore, and is a part of the advisory council for Agency: An Anarchist PR Project. Hillary lives in Pittsburgh, Pennsylvania.*

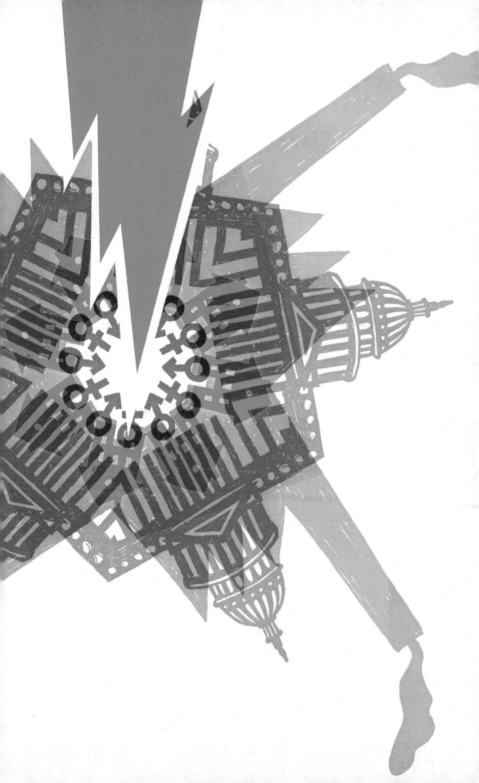

# STATE SANCTIONED
## VIOLENCE

# RAPE CULTURE

# ANTI-PATRIARCHAL ACTION

EXPLOITATION

ENVIRONMENTAL CATASTROPHIE

SYSTEMIC MURDER

WHITE SUPREMACY

HOMOPHOBIA

SOLIDARITY!

ANTI-RACIST WORK

MUTUAL AID

(A)

FEMINIST

AGAINST

PRISONS

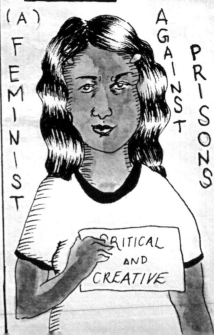

CRITICAL AND CREATIVE

# ABOLISHING THE "PSY"-ENCE FICTIONS: CRITIQUING THE RELATIONSHIP BETWEEN THE PSYCHOLOGICAL SCIENCES AND THE PRISON SYSTEM

## COLLEN HACKETT

Tiana is crying. She walks into the room, a large, powerful woman wearing a bland ensemble of a faded green top with similarly colored pants. The silent tears on her face are enough to quiet the many scattered conversations happening among us. Many of us try to make eye contact with Tiana, waiting for her to tell us what is wrong. She doesn't speak. She doesn't look at anyone. She sits and stares.

We're all sitting in a classroom in a women's prison. The space is filled with remedial educational materials for GED students, collages with magazine cutouts of models and vacation getaways, and clichéd motivational posters that inspire the incarcerated to become "ambitious" and "dedicated." In the moments of silence that follow Tiana's entrance, I'm reminded of the poster on the wall that lists the amendments to the US Constitution. On this poster the legendary constitutional change, the Thirteenth Amendment, only includes the part that formally abolishes slavery and does not include the part that says, "except as a punishment for crime whereof the party shall have been duly convicted." Every time I encounter suffering in that room, including my own,

« Art by Kristen Huizar

I remember that sterilized, whitewashed version of history hanging on the wall and cringe. And I rage, quietly.

Three other "outsiders" and I co-facilitate a class for survivors of intimate partner violence at a women's prison. Throughout this essay, I'll refer to "outsiders" and "insiders"—the chief distinction between the two labels is spatiality and refers to which side of the prison wall one resides on. The outsiders, including myself, are the nonincarcerated facilitators who go to the prison on a weekly basis and have been doing so for about two years. Our small, nonhierarchical collective of outsiders is made up of people who identify as women, artists, mamas, educators, scholars, and/or organizers, and most of us have histories of trauma, abuse, drug and alcohol misuse, or criminalization. The insiders are the incarcerated facilitators and participants who steer the curriculum and lead the popular-education-style classes. The people on the inside of the prison walls have less spatial and social freedoms than the outsiders, and the group makes every attempt possible to close this distance by centering the class's focal point on the voices, experiences, wisdom, and triumphs of the insiders.

We are based out of a prison in the Rocky West region that houses about a thousand people in various custody levels. As is typical in nearly all US prisons, there is a gross overrepresentation of Black, Brown, Native, and bi/multiracial peoples. This women's prison, much like other women's prisons, has a population with extremely high rates of reported and unreported trauma, past and/or ongoing physical and mental abuse, and sexual violence. There are estimations that 65-85 percent of people incarcerated in a women's jail or prison have histories of abuse compared to 30-45 percent abuse and sexual violence rates among non-incarcerated women.[1] Most of the people at this prison are poor. As many as 80 percent of those incarcerated at a women's prison meet the criteria for at least one psychiatric disorder. Many are mothers and a good majority are single mothers of children under eighteen, which can have devastating consequences for children, especially if they are funneled into the foster system. It is acutely clear that women's prisons contain a community of people who are at the lowest end of the social and economic strata: those who are considered disposable and expendable, those who have been historically debased by gendered and racialized violence as well as colonial conquest and aggressive neoliberal capitalism, and those who will suffer from the scarlet letter of incarceration. This scarlet letter or "mark" also signals other assumptions about a person to dominant society, branding the punished as inferior (biologically, culturally, or both), tainted, and irredeemable.

Social death, a concept most famously applied in describing the psychological effects of slavery in the US, is a consequence of the master's total control over a slave's body, labor, and identity.[2] The slave becomes wholly dependent upon the master after the social, genealogical, and historical alienation she experiences. In some instances, slaves who have experienced this sudden social death internalize a sense of zero self-worth, and adopt attitudes of blame and hate for the self and others who are like her. Although governmental and prison officials would like to obscure the direct similarities between the social death of slavery and the social death of prison, the parallels are striking. The manifestation of social death in the prison system is the ineligibility to personhood before, during, and after incarceration.[3] The very social institutions that claim to safeguard those who are the most "deserving" of protection have failed the women who find themselves in prison. Better-resourced and more-privileged women (oftentimes middle-class white women) benefit from domestic violence state services and the judicial system in ways that others do not. In contrast, the sex workers, the drug users and "addicts," the poor, the queer, the women of color, and the ones who were shut out of mainstream educational opportunities and legitimate economies are left to fend for themselves. These are the women whose bodies and localities bear signifiers of criminality, as judged by mainstream society and the court system, by being nonwhite and/or residing in disenfranchised and poverty-stricken neighborhoods. The legal system consequently becomes the master that attempts to strip women of their personhood. The criminal legal system sorts out the "real victims" from the "criminals." That is, women (and men, for that matter) who have simultaneously been harmed and have committed harm are not regarded as people with complex histories but rather as archetypal criminals with no "right" to helping services or freedom from institutionalized violence. Criminalized peoples are the disposable, the unworthy. The insidiousness of this social death process is the extent to which the myths of worthlessness have been absorbed into the stories that the incarcerated tell about themselves.

The outside facilitators bring programming into the women's facility to, at the very least, mitigate women's sense of social death. We ideally hope to mobilize prisoners' resistance to the brutally repressive circumstances in which they find themselves. In doing this, our class explores themes of oppression, power, and patriarchal and white supremacist violence, as well as liberation, resistance, and community organizing. The insiders frequently take the lead in facilitating healing circles in which prisoners voice their personal struggles and share insights and wisdom. Many of the class participants express that the act of articulating their problems helps to bring closure and lessen their pain. In addition to sharing our personal burdens, we also prioritize a politicized curriculum in which participants can connect these burdens to collective struggles. We have found that this process enhances our connectedness and empowers the group to think of ways to oppose and defend against domination. Our group often studies histories of struggle and people's movements for inspiration and proof that the so-called "power-less" are indeed brimming over with power and vitality. Our approach emphasizes the importance of merging the political and the personal, while honoring the resilience that we each hold. Therefore, we often operate within the messy confines of personal traumas, internalized oppression, and institutionalized violence that can lead to unexpected circumstances in the classroom. For example, our agenda on the next to last class was concerned with an organizing project to address the commissary markups at the facility (for instance, a ten cent bag of ramen sells for fifty cents), and we had not planned on Tiana's tears and need for support.

In our adoption of an anti-oppression praxis, we prioritize intersectional frameworks. This way of analyzing power is especially necessary for understanding the nuances of domination and how control is exercised through race, class, gender, sexuality, ableism, and citizenship, to name a few. The marriage of anarchism and feminism, particularly queer, women of color, and transnational feminisms, necessitates the dismantling of all oppressive structures. An essential part of this kind of revolutionary project demands that the interconnected structures of patriarchy, transnational capitalism, white supremacy, heteronormativity, and Western imperialism be recognized, as they act differently through and upon people with varied identities. Although traditionally, mainstream feminism has concerned itself with the struggle against gender oppression only and the differences between the "universal" categories of "women" and "men," a relevant feminist political project understands how other social markers and contexts trouble gender as a singular analytic category. As Sandra Harding points out, "There are no gender relations per se, but only gender relations as constructed by and between classes, races, and cultures."[4] I would add to this list: sexuality, ability, and legal status, which are particularly relevant when talking about incarcerated women. As Patricia Hill Collins has pointed out, these interlocking structures form a matrix of domination—the interconnection of race, class, gender, sexuality, age, nationality, and so on—that differentially, yet incisively, acts upon people depending upon where they are located in the power structure.[5]

The writings of Audre Lorde are acutely attuned to the varying ways in which the tools of domination operate on and through people. Lorde, especially in her exacting critiques of status quo (white, heterosexual, "first-world," class-advantaged) feminist theory, discusses the need to explore the personal as well as the political and never to separate the two.[6] Her radical feminist propositions had been preceded by Second Wave mainstream feminism a few years earlier, namely in the old adage of "the personal is political." That is, the experience of gendered oppression is one that is commonly ignored, laughed about, silenced, or dismissed. Lorde reminds white feminists in particular that their personal experiences cannot properly represent the daily manifestations of racialized and colonial violence that women of color personally experience. She proposes a radical and non-reformist framework through which, by adopting an intersectional politics, mainstream feminists might move away from their personal lives as women who benefit from the "master's tools [of domination and privilege]" and towards a critical consciousness of multitude, difference, and inclusivity. "Then, the personal as the political can begin to illuminate all our choices."[7] This illustrates the point that not only should the personal be political, but also that relevant political projects should make room for the "messiness" of our internal lives, and that there are multiple expressions of that "messiness."

The legacies of trauma, abuse, sexual assault, normalized violence, colonization, racist domination, and class war wreak havoc on our psychologies, to varying extents. There is no doubt that healing needs to happen (if it isn't already) at the individual and community level while we work to dismantle oppressive structures and ideologies. But so much of the management of that pain and social harm has been outsourced to a specialized professional class of psychiatrists, psychologists, and social workers who constitute an authoritative, unquestioned "psy-complex."[8] Surely there are effective healers and emotional laborers who find themselves entangled in and navigating the contentious terrain of the professional psy-complex. I know several well-intended social workers and therapists, many of them self-declared radicals, who do good work in either their private practice, or at a halfway house for folks with substance-dependence issues, or doing counseling with foster kids. I have no doubt that these individuals are amazingly helpful to the people they work with. It is not my intention to critique these individuals, but rather to turn my critical gaze towards the psy-complex structure that collaborates with governmental institutions and correctional facilities in ways that complement and enforce formalized systems of control.

The prison system in particular has used psychological evaluations and diagnostic categories of pathology as technologies of power for decades, establishing an obscured "psy"-ence fiction of criminality. In a typical psy-ence fiction, the story understands and talks about the individual *sans* social context; s/he/they lives in a vacuum and personal change is located in the mind of the individual. These psy-ence fictions try to tell us that criminalized people are those who fall victim to their own delusional mentalities and poor choices, instead of contextualizing criminal behaviors as those that are informed by disadvantage, social exclusion, necessity, and/or survival. Therefore, in any fully realized prison abolitionist or radical agenda, the political strategy must confront the more abstract technologies that control, manage, and subordinate populations. The abolitionist agenda, especially one that espouses anti-oppression intersectionalities, should also concern itself with the host of psy-ence fictions that attempt to regulate prisoners' mental worlds.

## CORRECTIONAL "TREATMENT" REGIMES

Despite the unplanned nature of Tiana's crisis, the group understood the need to put our organizing on hold, even though we have just two short hours of every week together, per prison policy. Incarcerated women live through so much unimaginable institutionalized and state-sanctioned violence that it would be difficult for an outsider facilitator to truly practice her emancipatory politics without exploring the personal. We ask Tiana if she wants to share or have us support her in some other way. Tiana wants to talk and she launches into a story about how she was degraded by a jealous "boy-girl" (prison slang for genderqueer or transman) on her way back to her cell. At 6 feet 1 inch, Tiana towers over most others at the prison and has learned to use intimidating body language as a defense mechanism. But that didn't work in this situation. The jealous boy-girl (X) stepped on Tiana's toes, called her a "stupid slut," and head-butted Tiana in her face. Tiana told us that she has not felt so degraded in a long time and, although she wanted to physically retaliate, she has two months left before she makes parole, and so she had to swallow her pride and restrain herself.

I've heard Tiana's story. As she puts it, she's a "rape baby." She is a biracial white and Black woman who, when growing up, had a lot of n-words thrown her way but was too light-skinned to fit in with the Black kids. She never felt like she fit in until she started rolling with the "big dog" gangsters. She was repeatedly used and abused by men on the outside. Tiana's personal history of gendered and racialized violence has sometimes left her silent, sometimes angry, and sometimes apathetic. But I've been amazed to see her use her powerful presence in our class to lead activities and to regularly talk about oppression and imagine structural alternatives. As Tiana increasingly steps into and owns her worth, she wants to know how she can transform her rage into political action—both on the inside and on the outside, once she's released.

Tiana continued to explain her story to the group and said that this confrontation set her back. That she was shaking with an overwhelming sense of being unworthy of anything good or righteous or powerful. Tiana walked away from the brief confrontation and tried to go on with her day as normal, and proceeded with her usual routine of going to the medication line. She saw her partner there, D. She didn't want to tell D about the incident, but word had already gotten around. Things like that usually make the gossip rounds fairly quickly. D asked Tiana what went down and after Tiana finished her story amidst periodic sobbing, X, the person in question, happened to be walking down the sidewalk toward the med line. Before Tiana could say or do anything, D was in a sprint towards X. D beat X down, badly. D was sent to the hole, and X was sent to the infirmary. Tiana is unsure that she'll see her boo, D, again before she is released.

As Tiana continued with her story, she laid bare her emotional complexities about the issue. She felt guilty. She thought that maybe if she didn't cry that hard that D would not have rushed to use physical violence against X. She felt sad. She didn't want to be released without seeing her primary support person again. And, she felt loved. Tiana said that she was so appreciative to have someone do something like that for her. Tiana said she's never had anyone "defend her honor" before. Most people in her life were too busy stepping on her to offer any kind of care for her. She also knows that D has never before beat anyone down on a lover's behalf. Tiana said she feels doubly honored that D, out of all people, would perform this kind of care for her in front of so many people.

At this point, I am itching to talk about the problems with lateral violence—violence enacted towards one's peers rather than towards the oppressors—and about the need to direct our fury towards the power structure and to treat each other with care. But the other outsiders and I hold our tongues. We don't interrupt Tiana's powerful confession of mixed emotions and appreciation for "honor" violence. For the duration of the class, both the insiders and the outsiders support her the best we can. We support each other in that moment, and I know that a conversation about lateral violence might come later, but it can't interrupt Tiana's immediate needs or be discussed in the future without also addressing institutional contexts. The prison, as a system and as a structure, is violent. And one would find it difficult to "live" within that system without embodying some aspect of that violence, that is, through developing internalized or externalized hatred, fear, disgust, or anger. Many of the women in our class tell us that they thought (or still think) that they were "crazy" to have angry, explosive reactions, and that they wish they were mentally strong enough to keep their cool in the face of extreme antagonism by other insiders or correctional staff. Most prison and psychiatric officials tell insiders that reacting to violence with violence is a personal choice that can be made or not made. In fact, prison facilities have a multitude of programming that advises prisoners on how to manage their unruliness—and to make "better" and "respectable" choices.

The emergence of the war on drugs and "tough-on-crime" politics of the 1980s and 1990s has, over the course of four decades, led to a globally unprecedented incarceration binge that destroys communities of color and communities living in poverty. This era of mass incarceration has led to an increase in prison and jail populations, while "crime" rates (officially defined) have been decreasing.9 The implementation of mandatory minimums and gender-neutral legislation coalesced to widen the net for women, despite a lack of increase in women's criminalized activity.[10] In just fifteen years, there has been a 400 percent overall increase in women's incarceration rates compared to a 200 percent increase in men's incarceration rates during the same time period.[11] By way of explanation, feminist historians have tracked the changes to the correctional system's patriarchal and paternalistic assumptions about femininity, womanhood, and domesticity. The Progressive Era of prison reform, between the mid-1800s and the 1950s, ushered in a peculiar kind of prison facility for women: the reformatory. Despite the variability in prison reformatory models across the

US, the common elements included an understanding of women's criminality as resulting from "madness" instead of "badness," and having "fallen from grace." Reformatories predominantly catered to younger white women (reserving for older white women and women of color the traditional prison system), and taught them skills to become more refined, more socially suitable, domesticated women. But as ideologies about women's offending began to shift, reformatories became outmoded.

In the crack-cocaine era of anti-Black discourses and politics, drug-using women across racial and ethnic categories became vilified, although to varying extents. The common understanding about women's criminality transformed into one that emphasized women's gender, sexual, and parental deviance—although this deviance was amplified in racialized ways. The state's use of the "welfare queen" and "female junkie" tropes hinged on the imagery of impoverished Black and Brown mothers in the inner city and their children (most commonly depicted as shaking premature infants who were falsely predicted to be a drain and a scourge on society). This narrative served to delegitimize welfare recipients' worthiness and to also scale back on welfare spending generally. During the same time period that legislators were gutting the welfare "nanny state," more resources were allocated to building prisons and ramping up the drug war and strengthening sentencing laws for violent crimes. This reconfiguration of the state channeled many women from the welfare system to the prison system. Media reports, official statements, and prison programming emphasized the irrational characteristics of a "new breed" of female deviant—in particular, their "manliness" and departure from the idealized archetype of womanhood. Considering that the net-widening prison system primarily targets women of color, poor women, sex workers, drug users, and single mothers, this understanding that women are not achieving a certain form of womanhood highlights the categorical use of hegemonic (mainstream white middle- and upper-class) femininity in correctional discourses. These racialized, classed, and gendered assumptions legitimate the increased policing and incarceration of women. They also carry over into psychological programming, classifying difference and disadvantage as pathological.

## THE PERSONAL IS POLITICAL; THE PERSONAL CAN BE MESSY; BUT THE PERSONAL SHOULD NOT BE PURELY PSYCHOLOGIZED

The "rehabilitative" and interventionist logics of correctional institutions have absorbed psychological systems of knowledge to construct "normal" people as those who abide by the law and use cool rationality to prevent or think their way out of potentially criminal situations. Therefore any person who might find herself in prison or in trouble with the law falls outside of the morally bound normative category of citizenship. A "good citizen" is one who adheres to laws and who generally aligns herself with ruling ideologies, including the adoption of the myth that citizens can use their psychological powers, such as "determination," to overcome "perceived" structural obstacles and discrimination. In the context of the prison, cognitive behavioral programs (a model that prisons are increasingly

adopting) urge prisoners to learn and adopt rational decision-making skills to avoid criminal thinking and illegal behaviors.[12] These programs attempt to normalize or habilitate prisoners and instill a sense of personal responsibility, with the assumption that women take little to no responsibility over their actions, blaming everything and everyone else for their poor choices.

These types of programs also hinge on unstated systems of morality. In traditional prison programming, the cognitive sciences have interestingly commingled with a dated, moralistic approach to changing prisoner populations. In Tiana's case, a psychiatrist or cognitive behavioral class facilitator presumably would have told her that having relations with another inmate is a violation of the prison rules, and that her involvement with an assault case stemmed from her overt infractions. But moreover, a cognitive behavioral class would have asked: Why did Tiana make the choice to tell D what X did to her? Why wouldn't Tiana make the better, more "healthy" choice of telling correctional staff that she was threatened and intimidated by another inmate? Why does Tiana feel loved because of a violent action? Why has Tiana made other bad choices in her life? Why is Tiana replicating the kind of criminal choices that landed her in prison in the first place? In these questions, the moralistic assumption is that Tiana has the freedom to make any kind of choice she wants to make, instead of understanding Tiana's agency as bounded by the power structure of the prison setting. The questions also try to imprint upon prisoners that they must ask for assistance from their masters—the correctional staff—rather than settling things among themselves and developing emotional autonomy from the psychological control complex. It is up to her to make the decision between "good" and "bad," "right" and "wrong," "legal" and "illegal," so long as it matches the official definitions. The covert implication of the doctrine of choice is that one can make a decision without the influence of violent institutional contexts, poverty, and histories of trauma, racism, and sexual violence. Yet having more "choices" in a structurally oppressive system typically signifies one's privileges and advantages within the system.

One of the more peculiar ways that prison programming is becoming liberalized and therefore legitimized is by way of "gender-responsiveness." Gender-responsiveness is a kind of approach that asserts that prisoners (and ex-prisoners) should receive treatment that takes into account how gender shapes one's past experiences in terms of emotional, physical, and sexual abuse and in terms of one's involvement in "illegitimate" economies. Prisons adopt gender-responsive models—so far, just in women's prisons—to claim that their staff and programming take into account the relationship between women's criminality and histories of trauma. Officials who use this model claim that it provides justice in a partially unjust system; they therefore try to soften the effects of a brutal prison regime for incarcerated women and to appease the critics. These programs use cognitive behavior therapies, described above, along with "empowerment" models, in which correctional staff members teach women how to lead productive lives. The focus in much of these therapeutic programs is on women's psychological health and how to emotionally overcome their past trauma. Social workers and therapists

(and in some cases, correctional officers) assert that the "fix" is less social and more psychological. To the authorities, outside circumstances don't have to change, but rather, "criminal" women have to stop their "stinkin' thinkin'," quit complaining, get more self-esteem, and play by the rules. The psy-complex defines empowerment in purely asocial and individualistic ways, measuring success by quantifying women's subjective skills like "positive thinking," and "having a constructive outlook." Therefore, if a woman has a "negative" attitude, officials believe she is not empowered to lead a future productive life, and she is then scapegoated for the very violence that the prison creates. Historical and structural oppressions become erased and invisibilized by status-quo psychological programming.

## TOWARDS A MORE LIBERATORY AND POLITICIZED PSYCHOLOGY

As prison abolitionists who have committed to bringing politicized education into the prison, we're enthusiastic about the idea of building resistance and organizing a movement inside a women's prison. I was incarcerated in my early twenties and, after my release, radical politics saved my life. It saved me from horribly abusive relationships with my partner (now ex-) and family members, and it saved me from a life of dissecting my psyche and asking the ill-informed question: why was I (and why am I) so messed up? In developing my own analysis of the world and of my life, it's clear that I acted based on my experiences in a terrorizing system; we all have to navigate an especially hostile world full of exploitation and domination, and sometimes that means some folks, like myself, resort to a syringe full of heroin day in and day out to escape. And since radical politics, particularly anarchism, saved my life, why wouldn't a structural analysis help folks like Tiana, or others at the women's prison, who might be struggling with victim blaming and shame?

But it soon became clear that a purely political education doesn't help with all of the pains that someone struggling with mental health issues has, or that someone who bears the burden of losing her children to the foster care system has. In touting critical analyses as the cure, I must have had a selective memory of what things got me through my time locked down and after my release: friends, music, mutual-aid–based self-help groups like AA, nature, and the structural supports that accompany white privilege. We immediately felt the disconnect between what the outsiders wanted—wanting to talk about organizing and the connection between heteropatriarchy, white supremacy and domestic violence—and what the insiders wanted: to never be in an abusive relationship again (and in some cases, to get out of the abusive relationship they are currently in); to relieve the suffering of prison life; and to better connect with family and supporters on the outside. We failed to recognize or remember the immediacy of many of the needs in the room, which prompted a collective reflection, including on the part of insiders, on how we might build a class together that can achieve a better union of the personal and the political.

Ignacio Martín-Baró, a Jesuit priest, scholar, and activist assassinated by the Salvadoran army in 1989 for his anti-authoritarian views and his

scholarship on liberation, argued that the sociopolitical and the individual are inseparable. Moreover, he argues that any psychological endeavor must move beyond the personal and incorporate a community-and structural-level analysis. Inspired by Paulo Freire and the conceptual development of oppression in South and Central America during the 1960s and 1970s, Martín-Baró contended that developing a critical consciousness, or *concientización*, of how power and oppression operate to suppress dissent and total freedom was a necessary step in liberation. He writes that the "awakening of critical consciousness joins the psychological dimension of personal consciousness with its social and political dimension,"[13] and further argues that understanding the personal would be "incomprehensible" if the social structural reference points were omitted. Therefore, avoiding discussions of the psychological effects of oppression can lead to alienation; personal experiences should be considered a necessary part of organizing relevant political projects.

Healing from the psychological wounds that are inflicted by daily acts of violence, microaggressions, and systematic degradations demands that we critically understand power structures and work to transform them. The cycle of liberation is one that incorporates the personal, the community, and the social, and honors the interconnectedness between them. "Recovering the historical memory"[14] and reclaiming cultures are necessary projects for providing psychological support and political momentum, yet mainstream psychologists (and other "experts," for that matter) have ignored these needs. This violent ignorance (and at times blatant suppression) arises when psychologists are incorporated into the "professional" stratum in which they hold positions of power or work for powerful authority figures, instead of working for the people they claim to serve. The psycomplex experts are not interested in directing attention to much outside of the patient's mind because, to psychologists, we cannot control the outside world; we can only control our reactions and our perspectives.

A radical political analysis should not only directly refute this individualistic take on social problems, but it should also prioritize the needs, desires, and interests of the group or set of individuals seeking psychological healing. For oppressed and exploited peoples who are subject to monitoring and psychological evaluation through the prison system, I contend that developing networks of mutual aid and support are more empowering than outsourcing our psychological grievances to specialized experts. In our prison class for survivors of intimate partner violence, we focus on a cycle of liberation that includes specific strategies to heal the personal, nurture the intrapersonal, and engage with the political. In personal terms, we nourish our psyches by validating each other's feelings, encouraging self-exploration in terms of sexuality and identity supporting self-care, and promoting artistic expression. We recognize the valuable qualities of courage and resiliency that women already hold in the room.

In finding liberatory possibilities on the intrapersonal level, working within a prison setting can be especially difficult and challenging. Violent institutions breed resistance, but they also sometimes breed hostility,

backstabbing, horizontal divisions, and gossiping among people who are similarly oppressed. In our class, this means that there is an initial growing period in which new participants who might have been unfriendly with each other join the outsiders and the more experienced insiders in finding our common struggles and our empathy for the struggles we have not experienced. This solidarity-building is especially effective in exploring the controlling dynamics of the prison administration and how each person experiences this power regime. We sometimes do this by using Theatre of the Oppressed activities in which participants can role-play oppressive dynamics that they may have experienced or witnessed and brainstorm how, if at all, the oppressive "character" can be undermined or resisted. In developing a sense of community with each other, we also better nurture individual expressions and feed our psychological needs. Using improvisational body movements and writing poetry or essays often helps to facilitate different ways to use voice. And, if the personal and the intrapersonal reveal existing commonalities, discussing the political becomes an exciting exploration of strategies for action and organizing.

In assessing our personal-is-political projects, especially in a women's prison, we must broaden our ideas of what is political, so as to also understand how acts of resistance are wide-ranging and not simply reducible to a prison riot or hunger strike. Victoria Law has produced great documentation of how we can think about and classify resistance in women's prisons.[15] A behavior is political when it confronts oppression and supports class and group interests, meaning that refusing to stay silent, filing grievances, and supporting each other are all political acts. When Tiana, for example, asks for emotional solace and a dozen women on the inside put their organizing projects on hold to cry and laugh with her and tell her that she is loved despite the messiness of the situation, the act is a political one.

## NOTES

1    The National Intimate Partner and Sexual Violence Survey: 2010 Summary Report.

2    Orlando Patterson, *Slavery and Social Death: A Comparative Study* (Cambridge, MA: Harvard Press, 1982).

3    Lisa Marie Cacho, *Social Death: Racialized Rightlessness and the Criminalization of the Unprotected* (New York, NY: New York University Press, 2012).

4    Sandra Harding, *Whose Science? Whose Knowledge?: Thinking From Women's Lives* (Ithaca, NY: Cornell University Press, 1991), 171.

5    Patricia Hill Collins, *Black Feminist Thought: Knowledge, Consciousness, and the Politics of Empowerment* (New York, NY: Routledge, 2000).

6    Audre Lorde, *Sister Outsider: Essays and Speeches* (Berkeley, CA: Crossing Press, 2007).

7    Ibid, 114.

8    Shoshanna Pollack, "Taming the Shrew: Regulating Prisoners through Women-Centered Mental Health Programming" in *Critical Criminology*, (`2005) 13: 71-87.

9    The Sentencing Project: Research and Advocacy for Reform. http://www.sentencingproject.org.

10    Jill McCorkel, *Breaking Women: Gender, Race, and the New Politics of Imprisonment* (New York, NY: New York University Press, 2013).

11    The Sentencing Project.

12    Kelley Hannah-Moffat, "Criminogenic Need and the Transformative Risk Subject: Hybridizations of Risk/Need in Penality" in *Punishment and Society*, 2004 7(1):29-51.

13    Ignacio Martín-Baró, *Writings for a Liberation Psychology* (Cambridge, MA: Harvard University Press, 1994), 18.

14    Ibid.

15    Victoria Law, *Resistance Behind Bars: The Struggles of Incarcerated Women* (Oakland, CA: PM Press, 2012).

## ABOUT THE AUTHOR

*Colleen Hackett (firehawk) is an ex-con, writer, educator, and organizer. With a few unruly outsiders and many exuberant insiders, she cofounded Webs of Support, a prison program led by incarcerated women who have experienced intimate partner violence. She's also involved in a new antiauthoritarian prisoner publication,* Unstoppable!, *which is by and for prisoners who identify as women, gendervariant, or trans (unstoppable. noblogs.org). She lives with her dog in the desert and enjoys tae bo, bicycling, and deep-eco-pagan-metal.*

Art by N.O. Bonzo

# COMING TO TERMS: RETHINKING POPULAR APPROACHES TO FEMINISM AND ANARCHISM

## THERESA WARBURTON

To save our movements, we need to come to terms with the connections between gender violence, male privilege, and the strategies that informants...use to destabilize radical movements...Despite all that we say to the contrary, the fact is that radical social movements and organizations in the United States have refused to seriously address gender violence as a threat to the survival of our struggles.
—Courtney Desiree Morris, "Why Misogynists Make Great Informants: How Gender Violence on the Left Enables State Violence in Radical Movements"

How is it that revolutionary libertarian fervor can exist so harmoniously with machismo? It is far too easy in this instance to say that "it is hard to locate our tormentor. It's so pervasive, so familiar. We have known it all our lives. It is our culture." Because...the essences of liberty so illustriously espoused by these people have not extended their definition of freedom to their sisters.
—Ruby Flick, "Anarcha-Feminism"

The relationship between anarchism and feminism is a peculiar one. Though there has been exponential interest in anarchist movements, theory, and studies in the past twenty years, this increase has not necessarily led to an expanse of writing or theorizing on the relationship between anarchism and feminism.

While feminism has become a deep enough concern that most contemporary anarchist texts make mention of it in one way or another, there have been very few texts dedicated solely to this question. The most prominent among them is a new expanded edition of the formative collection, *Quiet Rumours: An Anarcha-Feminist Reader.*

Though many online articles and pamphlets from women and queer people, as well as myriad personal accounts and reports, insist that feminism is necessary in anarchist movements, the crushing reality of gendered violence in radical antiauthoritarian communities has yet to be adequately addressed.[1] How might our approach to the relationship between anarchism and feminism be related to the continuing problem of gendered violence within radical communities? And how might we re-envision it in creative, productive ways?

Let us slow down a minute, though, and be clear about some terms. At the crux of this discussion is the presence of gendered violence in radical communities in the US. "Radical communities" is a relatively loose term for interactive spaces of the radical Left committed to antiauthoritarian organizing methods and ideas.[2] Sometimes, these are intentional groups of people organized around a particular geographic location; sometimes, they might be virtual spaces where people come together to discuss particular issues or political tendencies. Unfortunately, the problem of gendered violence is widespread enough in a variety of communities organized around radical antiauthoritarian politics that we can see similar forms of it operating despite widely varying locations, intentions, and histories.

"Gendered violence" includes a range of forms of violence exercised in order to enforce the gender binary (and the structures of power from which it is formed), the most prominent examples being sexual and domestic violence, sexual harassment, and discrimination on the basis of gender identity, gender expression, or sexual preference. Taking as central the work of many feminists of color, we should work against the notion that this is strictly a form of interpersonal violence and reiterate at the outset that gendered violence is a form of systemic violence that is directly and intimately bound up in other institutionalized forms of violence, including capitalism, white supremacy, and colonialism.[3] Of particular concern is how contemporary approaches to the relationship between anarchism and feminism normalize gendered violence within radical communities that are created in order to confront structures and institutions of oppression.

Perhaps one of the strongest contentions that prevent a critical engagement with the reality of gendered violence in radical communities is the simple fact that these spaces do not exist in an insulated place apart from mainstream society. This fact is often upheld as an explanation for the presence of gendered violence in radical spaces, since coming into such a space does not immediately undo dominant types of socialization.[4] And this is fair enough, since it does help reckon with the presence of overarching structures of institutional and interpersonal violence in spaces meant to confront them. However, we run into trouble when this logic becomes an excuse rather than an attempt to take a truly radical approach, or one that seeks to understand where and how it is rooted. Because, while it is true that these communities do not exist outside of those dominant forms of social organization, this reasoning does not account for the fact that these communities are supposed to be grounded in radical commitments that would begin to eradicate these forms of violence, rather than enable them.

To gain a sense of the prevalence of these forms of violence just talk to most anyone who is not a cisgender male of any radical community and you'll likely hear an unending series of stories that run the gamut of violent behavior, from everyday microaggressions, including misogynistic and transphobic comments, to outright acts of physical and mental abuse.

These attitudes and practices become normalized using the logic and language of radicalism. For example, we can look to the particular ways hypermasculinity prevalent in radical spaces mutates the promotion of direct action into a valorization of violence. We can also see how a lack of community-based accountability processes, combined with pressure not to disclose abuse and assault to other community members, local antiviolence organizations, or state agents, creates conditions where there are no ramifications for gendered violence.[5] And even when there are accountability mechanisms, cis men often function as gatekeepers, creating accountability processes in which those who are most harmed by gendered violence are not in control of the structures used to address it. In each of these examples, we can see how radical ideals provide spaces for gendered violence to flourish rather than reducing its negative impacts.

So what does this have to do with the contemporary relationship between anarchism and feminism? The reality of gendered violence in radical communities seems to be one of the most salient questions that an engagement with feminism should help anarchism address. However, it is one that is often cautiously ignored or rerouted to more hushed, private discussions to be had internally within particular organizations. Perhaps in a world that can be hostile to anarchism itself, it can feel dangerous to talk about the problems within our communities for fear of providing fodder to critics. However, it is infinitely more dangerous to ignore the continued challenges of those of us who experience and witness not only the effects, but the perpetuation of heteropatriarchy within radical communities, especially since ignoring the problem ends up adding weight to critiques that suggest anarchism is incapable of providing real-world solutions to broad-based problems of domination. This trend might also be replicated in contemporary theoretical approaches to anarchism and feminism.

There are three overarching trends in discussions of anarchism and feminism. Here I emphasize the benefits of each while suggesting various limitations. These approaches include the genealogical approach, the equivalent approach, and the exchange approach. The typical approaches have helped us better understand the history of feminist anarchists and anarchist feminists (the genealogical approach); the traits and practices that are shared by them both historically and today (the equivalent approach); and what they might be able to learn from each other (the exchange approach). However, these approaches have prevented us from addressing a crucial question that underlies the continued push for feminist praxis in anarchist spaces:

how do misogyny, heteropatriarchy, and transphobia become normalized within anarchist theories and practices? Each fails to pay attention, however, to one of the most significant advances in feminist scholarship of the past twenty years: the employment of feminism as a critical methodology and praxis; that is, as a body of work that enables us to contend with the ways in which gendered and sexualized forms of institutionalized violence are not only intertwined with, but incorporated into, a variety of social, political, and cultural structures and spaces. This method is based on the work of feminists of color who have consistently demonstrated the necessity of this approach, using it to apprehend feminism itself.[6]

Understanding the structure of the dominant approaches is essential here because it helps answer the question not only of what the relationship between anarchism and feminism is, but why it has historically taken these shapes. That is, what questions has the conversation surrounding the relationship been seeking to answer? That is, how are these structures supported within anarchist spaces, using anarchist logics, rather than just as imports from mainstream society?

## THE GENEALOGICAL APPROACH

One of the most popular methods of approaching the relationship between anarchism and feminism is the genealogical approach. In this approach, the focus is on establishing a history of anarchist feminist thinkers, often presented chronologically. While each version of this approach may vary in what politics it highlights in its survey of thinkers, what they have in common is the goal of creating a distinct history of anarchist feminist thought. This genealogy provides the architecture for popular engagements, such as the collection *Quiet Rumours*, which features writings from anarchist feminist thinkers spanning the nineteenth to the twenty-first centuries.[8]

In her chapter on The Anarchist Turn, entitled "Of What is Anarcha-Feminism the Name?," Cinzia Arruzza employs this genealogical model in her attempt to articulate "the peculiar aspects of the critique of women's oppression" in early anarchist feminist texts in order to establish how "these aspects coalesce to produce an original view that anticipates Second Wave feminism." Here, Arruzza lays out the genealogy of anarchist feminist thought, moving from late nineteenth century writers Emma Goldman and Voltairine de Cleyre to mid-twentieth century writers like Carol Ehrlich, Peggy Kornegger, Lynne Farrow, and Marian Leighton, ending in the late twentieth and early twenty-first century influences of poststructuralist feminism, queer theory, and ecofeminism.[9]

Understanding this genealogy has proven important for understanding anarchist feminism as a distinct and (relatively) cohesive theoretical tradition, especially since this genealogy provides a formulation that exists alongside and within the history of anarchism, rather than arising as an ancillary concern. In the best case, this approach is useful in that it helps to establish a history of thinkers who understood how deeply intertwined gendered and class violence were in the time that they were writing. This is important in that it helps demonstrate that the question of gendered oppression has been a part of anarchism for at least a century, rather than a contemporary development. In the worst case, however, this approach is used to dispel any criticism of misogyny or heteropatriarchy in anarchist spaces or history by holding up particular individual anarchist feminists as tokens.[10] Instead of using the history of anarchist feminist thinkers to argue for considering gendered oppression as a central concern, this latter case disposes of the need for such a discussion by replacing a concerted effort to understand the intersections of gendered and class systems with a representational model of integration that effectively denies the existence of such systems in the first place.

Of course, this is not to argue that we should do away with this approach simply because there are people who abuse it in order to neglect the material effects of gendered and sexualized hierarchies. Rather, the slippage between the best and worst case scenarios highlight a structural problem in the approach itself that prevents it from adequately articulating an inherent opposition to the gendered and sexualized hierarchies upon which misogyny and heteropatriarchy depend. That is, both in theory and in practice, the approach of laying out a genealogy does not intrinsically work against the presence of gendered and sexualized hierarchies within contemporary anarchist spaces. Instead, it provides a genealogy of critiques of dominant society from an anarchist feminist perspective that can be mobilized to direct attention away from self-critique.

In this way, a genealogical approach is not effective for addressing sexual violence in contemporary radical communities. This is for reasons that affect both the structure and content of anarchist feminist history, as well as its

influence on the contemporary moment. In the simplest terms, this is a matter of direction. The genealogical approach, in both structure and content, often places anarchist feminisms alongside anarchism more broadly, looking out.[11] Thus, the history provided by the genealogical approach provides a grounded analysis of how anarchist feminist writers have critiqued the gendered and sexualized stigmas of dominant society. However, it doesn't necessarily help us understand the legacies of sexual violence in anarchist communities or how people have resisted them. Nor does it help us understand how hierarchical structures have become normalized within those spaces to such an extent that they continue to be a prominent issue in communities that profess a rejection of the structures through which such violence in constructed and maintained.

## THE EQUIVALENT APPROACH

The limitations of the genealogical approach are, in some ways, mirrored in the equivalent approach that became popular in the mid-twentieth century. Exemplified by Peggy Kornegger's 1975 pamphlet "Anarchism: The Feminist Connection," the equivalent approach articulates the relationship between anarchism and feminism as one of interchangeability. As Kornegger famously argued, "It is my contention that feminists have been unconscious anarchists in both theory and practice for years."[12] Lynn Farrow echoed this sentiment the same year when she argued that "feminism practices what anarchism preaches," as did Marian Leighton the next year when she argued that "the refining distinction from radical feminist to anarcho-feminist is largely that of making a step in self-conscious theoretical development."[13] We can see expressed in these examples differentiated expressions of the same core values and practices.

This approach has proven important for emphasizing the theoretical consistency across the rejection of hierarchy by anarchists and the rejection of heteropatriarchy by feminists. In this way, the equivalent approach attempts to preclude the existence of a nonfeminist anarchism while also arguing that women are particularly well positioned for anarchist practice, echoing developing articulations of a Marxist feminist epistemology that arose a few years later in the early 1980s.[14] Kornegger described feminists of the time as "intuitive anarchists" which, according to her, put "women in the unique position of being the bearers of a subsurface anarchist consciousness which...can take us further than any previous group toward the achievement of total revolution."[15] This approach, then, attempts not only to highlight a theoretical equivalence but also to articulate the practical results of such a theoretical intervention. The danger of this approach, however, is related to its most important contribution—the preclusion of the existence of a nonfeminist anarchism. By articulating anarchism and feminism as equivalent, this model prevents an engagement with anarchism using a critical feminist lens that aims to expose the practical affinities that anarchists have found between anarchism and heteropatriarchy, leading to its continued presence in anarchist spaces.

The limitations of using this approach in order to attend to the sustained existence of sexual violence in radical communities are similar, then, to those discussed in terms of the genealogical approach. Again, this method doesn't allow for an understanding of anarchism as a space where, for whatever reasons, the social, cultural, and political bases for sexual violence remain intact, reified by radical principles. It's not that these reasons are not important, but rather, they are hidden by this approach; as a result, we lack a substantial body of work that helps understand what these reasons are, where they come from, and how they are maintained. In this approach, feminism and anarchism are enacted as equivalent forms of radical resistance, divesting from feminism its critical possibilities.

Foregrounding equivalence, rather than the critical potential of feminism for anarchism, this approach to anarchist feminism creates the illusion that anarchism and feminism are inherently synonymous. Though this approach has been important in emphasizing the similarities, it also prevents the use of feminism as a critical lens through which to assess how heteropatriarchal structures become normalized within anarchist theory and practice. This critical feminist assessment of anarchism seems essential to understanding how sexual violence proliferates not only in radical communities, but also through the actions of radical people, including those who are sincerely committed to nonhierarchical and antiauthoritarian principles. It is not enough to simply argue that sexual violence committed by radical people is merely a result of a continuing infection of dominant ideas that bleed into radical communities. Rather, we must be honest about the fact that, for many of these people, the violence that occurs may not, to them, seem out of line with their radical principles.

The equivalent approach precludes this type of inquiry by articulating anarchism and feminism as not only theoretically unified but also inherently synonymous in practice. What is more, this approach also precludes a more developed discussion of how certain forms of feminism also end up reifying structures of oppression, ranging from radical feminist investments in transphobia to liberal feminist investments in the state.[16] Within the equivalent model, feminism becomes synonymous with a very particular rendition of radical feminism. Such an approach hinders our ability to critically assess feminism as well as anarchism, preventing us from seeing a fuller picture of how certain forms of feminism have been, and continue to be, complicit not only with state power and capitalism, but also with gendered violence.

## THE EXCHANGE APPROACH

The attempt to rectify this limitation is central to the exchange approach that characterizes most of the contemporary writing on anarchism and feminism. In recent years, numerous writers have attempted to account for the diversity of feminist thought in their discussions of the relationship between anarchism and feminism. Articles like J. Rogue and Deric Shannon's "Refusing to Wait: Anarchism and Intersectionality," and Abbey Volcano and J. Rogue's "Insurrection at the Intersection: Feminism, Intersectionality, and Anarchism," destabilize this monolithic engagement with feminism in order to emphasize the work of feminists of color. For instance, drawing on the notion of "intersectionality" first named by Black feminist legal scholar Kimberlé Crenshaw, Shannon and Rogue argue that "anarchists could learn a lot" from feminists of color, especially "about the importance of addressing the needs of ALL sections of the working class and their attempts to check the tendency of the Left to ignore or dismiss the concerns, needs, ideas, and leadership of people living in the dangerous intersections of capitalism, white supremacy, patriarchy, etc."

Drawing on the work of INCITE! Women of Color Against Violence, a "national activist organization of radical feminists of color advancing a movement to end violence against women of color and our communities through direct action, critical dialogue, and grassroots organizing," Rogue and Shannon bring the critiques that feminists of color had of white liberal feminism to bear on contemporary anarchism. Similarly, Volcano and Rogue use the example of radical approaches to reproductive freedom to demonstrate why anarchists must incorporate an approach to feminism that recognizes the multiple ways that "capitalism, white supremacy, and heteropatriarchy... have required control over bodies"—a control that has been differentially enacted upon the bodies of women of color and queer folks. Echoing the work of feminist writers Andrea Smith and Dorothy Roberts, Volcano and Rogue argue for "an anarchist intersectional analysis of reproductive freedom" that can account for the differential ways that people experience both the restrictions of their reproductive freedom as well as the structure and content of their movements to fight against these restrictions.[17] In both of these cases, contemporary anarchist writers attend to the important interventions of feminists of color in order to reconfigure the approach in a way that recognizes not only the diversity of feminist thought, but also the critical potential of feminism as well.

However, there is also an important limitation to the exchange approach. In particular, this approach is often predicated on the idea of a bidirectional exchange enabled through a process of synthesis. As Rogue and Shannon put it, "We firmly believe that this learning process is a two-way street." Because of this, they argue that "when synthesizing our practice to include these concerns raised by feminists, feminism could stand to benefit from learning from anarchism as well." This method is echoed in Volcano and Rogue's article, which attempts to use a synthetic method to develop an "anarchist intersectionality," as well as in the collection *Queering Anarchism: Addressing and Undressing Power and Desire*, the introduction of which is titled "Queer Meet Anarchism, Anarchism Meet Queer." In these formulations, the presumption is not only that anarchism needs feminism, but that feminism needs anarchism, as well. And, of course, there are many instances in which this seems to be the case—for instance, in the case of trans-exclusive feminism or in schools of feminist thought that look to the state for liberation, and which see advanced class status as an indication of progress against gendered oppression.[18]

However, this element of the exchange approach is limited in its implication that feminisms of color, in particular, require the influence of anarchism. Rogue and Shannon argue that "anarchism can provide a radical base from which to critique liberal interpretations of intersectionality," as well as "a

critical analysis of the state." But it is not clear why feminists of color would need anarchism to provide a "critical analysis of the state," as Shannon and Rogue note, when such an analysis is often central to the feminism they espouse. For instance, INCITE!, the organization from which Rogue and Shannon draw their analysis, is expressly antistate, arguing for an understanding of sexual violence that views it as one example of statist violence enacted through systems of colonialism and militarism.

What is more, while anarchism is grounded in a political method of prefiguration that moves beyond a critique of the state in order to envision social organization outside of nation-states, there has been no engagement with Native thinkers that moves beyond their inclusion in lists of ethno-racial groups. Compelling alternatives to the nation-state exist throughout hundreds of Native tribes and nations on this land, who demonstrate alternative modes of social organization prior to the establishment of the US nation-state in particular, as well as the nation-state structure in general—modes which continue to this day, as Native peoples enact and fight for sovereignty and self-determination.[18] What each of these examples demonstrate is not that there is nothing that Native feminists and feminists of color have in common with anarchists (or that there may not be people who see themselves as part of both groups) but rather that Native feminists and feminists of color have historically come to their own critiques of the state and capitalism, as well as visions for alternative methods of social organization, through different genealogies than those of anarchists. That is, though not all feminists of color and

Native feminists have offered an anti-capitalist and antistate analysis, there are certainly enough that it remains questionable that these thinkers would need to turn to anarchism for these critical analyses. Because of this, any approach to anarchism and feminism should affirm these differing genealogies, concurring with the insistence of Native feminists and feminists of color that they can explain and resist their own oppression best on their own terms.

The limitations of the exchange approach for dealing with sexual violence within radical communities stem from a lack of this affirmation, grounded in the misassumption of a bidirectional exchange between the two bodies of thought. In the simplest terms, we cannot assume that feminists, particularly Native feminists and feminists of color, must be required to take something from anarchism in exchange for their critical interventions. Sexual violence is a problem that, regardless of politics, is predominantly perpetrated by white men and has the strongest negative impact on women and queer folks of color.[19] This is a problem that is often replicated in radical communities and, in our attempt to better articulate the relationship between anarchism and feminism, we can't ignore the presence of this unequal relationship. That is, because sexual violence in radical communities disproportionately affects women and queer folks, especially those of color, we can't assume that intellectual exchange between feminism and anarchism, a body of theory that is still dominated by white male thinkers, should be bidirectional either. This isn't to say that anarchism has nothing to offer feminists, necessarily. Rather, we would need to be very clear about what it is that anarchism brings to the table that hasn't

already been put forward by women of color and Native women critiquing mainstream feminism. As it stands, it isn't clear what this intervention would be.[20]

## CONCLUSION

Attending to a different framing of the relationship between anarchism and feminism is paramount because of the very real, material effects that sexual violence has on particular populations within and without radical spaces. This is a need that continues to be reasserted, as instances of sexual and gendered violence seem to be woven into the fabric of radical resistance in the US. As Morris notes, "Gender violence has historically been deeply entrenched in the political practices of the Left and constituted one of the greatest (if largely unacknowledged) threats to the survival of these organizations." This is both because it enables certain members of radical communities to enact violence on others with impunity, and because it enables agents of state repression, such as informants, to exploit those weaknesses as well. Luft makes a similar observation in her piece, "Looking for Common Ground: Relief Work in Post-Katrina New Orleans as an American Parable of Race and Gender Violence," highlighting how instances of gendered violence in a particular radical community pushed a foundationally antiracist organization to mutate the logic of their radical politics in ways that are "almost generic" as a "discrete example of sexism and violence."[21] Both emphasize the detrimental effects not just for survivors, but also for the movements of which they are a part. As Morris notes, "Radical movements cannot afford the destruction that gender violence creates," because "if we underestimate the political implications of patriarchal behaviors on our communities, the work will not survive."[22]

Each approach is predicated on the question of how we might consider anarchism and feminism together. The result is that each attempts to articulate the positive connections between these two bodies of thought: the genealogical approach attempts to highlight individual thinkers throughout history who have built the anarchist feminist tradition; the equivalent approach argues that anarchism and feminism are not only similar, but synonymous; and the exchange approach suggests that anarchists and feminists must come together to create a synthesis of the two that is grounded in principles of bidirectional influence. Each of these approaches has provided useful contributions, both theoretical and practical. However, we need to move beyond these approaches to ask the more complicated question that undergirds the persistence of gendered violence in anarchist communities: what is the relationship between anarchism and heteropatriarchy, misogyny, and transphobia?

Addressing this question requires understanding feminism as a method or praxis through which to practice self-critique, rather than only as a body of analysis. Though self-critique is not entirely absent from Leftist movements, few have integrated it as an intrinsic part of the movement as deeply as feminist movements of the past forty years. In a recent interview, Black anticapitalist feminist bell hooks discusses this as a core reason for her continued identification with feminism, despite its problems:

My militant commitment to feminism remains strong, and the main reason is that feminism has been the contemporary social movement that has most embraced self-interrogation. When we, women of color, began to tell white women that females were not a homogenous group, that we had to face the reality of racial difference, many white women stepped up to the plate. I'm a feminist in solidarity with white women today for that reason, because I saw these women grow in their willingness to open their minds and change the whole direction of feminist thought, writing and action. This continues to be one of the most remarkable, awesome aspects of the contemporary feminist movement.[23]

For hooks, this is one of the core elements of feminist praxis that makes it distinct from other radical Left movements and thought. It is this vision of feminist praxis that is missing from the approaches that I described above.

To be sure, emphasizing the contradictions of a nonfeminist anarchism, or one that does not recognize the fight against gendered structures of oppression in its rejection of hierarchy, is a necessary project. Likewise, so is emphasizing the places where these bodies of work intersect. However, such work does not help us understand how those structures become manifest in radical communities, using radical political logic and language. As Ruby Flick points out in one of the epigraphs to this piece, it is too easy an answer to merely say that gendered oppression, including gendered violence, in radical communities is only a result of their presence within a system where heteropatriarchy is omnipresent. Rather, we must ask the more difficult question of how we can come to terms with not only the presence but also the tacit sanctioning of gendered violence that is enabled through our failure to address how it becomes rooted and reinforced using radical principles.

This question is much more difficult both to accept and to address. It's an uncomfortable question, because it requires that we critically assess anarchism and its limitations—something that can feel very dangerous in a world where anarchism carries such negative connotations and is often misrepresented in truly disfiguring ways. The title to this piece, "Coming to Terms," is used to invoke the process of addressing this question because it underscores two related practices that are essential to developing a transformative approach to anarchism and feminism that is capable of addressing the persistence of gendered violence in radical communities. First, we must come to terms in the sense that we must acknowledge the presence of gendered violence in the particular forms that both its exercise and its defense take in radical communities. This first coming to terms might be understood as a form of mourning, a time to be vulnerable in recognizing the limitations of our practice so far. Second, we must come to terms in the sense of developing new terms for engaging the relationship between anarchism and feminism. This second coming to terms might be understood as a form of architectural rebuilding, a time to create a new foundational structure from which to develop the discussion itself.

Both of these forms of coming to terms are important. Though it might feel risky to engage in the type of self-critique that makes anarchism vulnerable to outside condemnation, avoiding it is even more dangerous. We risk turning our backs on those in our communities who are most affected by the forms of violence we seek to dismantle; we risk ignoring the contributions of those who come to similar analyses of power from different genealogies and histories than ours; and we risk attempting to create equal relationships through ideology, rather than through material changes in people's everyday lives. With this in mind, this piece is not an answer to the question of how to deal with gendered violence in radical communities. Rather, it is a gesture toward possible approaches, both intellectual and practical, through which we might enable ourselves to struggle together in finding new answers.

## NOTES

1    For some examples of work that describes the presence of gendered violence in these communities, see Zabalaza Books, eds. *A Collection of Essays on Feminism and Sexism in the Anarchist Movement* (South Africa: Zabalaza Books, 2015)

2    Here, I use the terms *antiauthoritarian* and *anarchist* relatively interchangeably, though I understand that anarchism, depending on the tradition, is not always conceptualized this way. In this way, I am gesturing towards the issue of gendered violence not only in self-identified anarchist spaces, but also in spaces that invoke antiauthoritarian political principles, particularly an anticapitalist and antiracist platform that is grounded in a rejection of all forms of hierarchy, and antiauthoritarian organizational principles, like the use of affinity groups, consensus-based decision

making, direct democracy, and noncarceral accountability processes.

3    For examples of these feminist accounts of gendered violence as an institutional form, see: Sarah Deer, *The Beginning and End of Rape: Confronting Sexual Violence in Native America*. (Minneapolis, University of Minnesota Press, 2015).

4    These types of socialization include hypersexualization, racialized discourses about sexuality such as the myth of the Black rapist, and the normalization of sexual violence enabled through practices like victim blaming, lack of consent, and harmful understandings of aggressive masculinity.

5    In 2004, the National Sexual Violence Resource Center reported that men are more likely to commit sexual violence in communities where sexual violence goes unpunished.

6    See Amanda Lock Swarr and Richa Nagar, eds, 2012. *Critical Transnational Feminist Praxis* (Albany, SUNY Press, 2012).

7    I use the terms misogyny, heteropatriarchy, and transphobia in tandem here in order to give shape to the myriad forms of gendered violence. From my perspective, none of these terms alone accounts for all these forms, though these terms indelibly intersect.

8    Throughout, I will use the term *anarchist feminism* rather than anarcha- or anarcho-feminism. I do this in order to enable me to use the same term throughout, even in cases where the type of synthetic approach that the terms *anarcha-* or *anarcho-feminism* imply.

9    Cinzia Arruzza, "Of What is Anarcha-Feminism the Name?" in Jacob Blumenfeld, Chiara Bottici, and Simon Critchley. eds. *The Anarchist Turn*, (New York: Pluto Books, 2013), 113. It should be noted that this genealogy follows the popular "Wave" genealogy of feminism more broadly, a trend that has been critiqued by feminists.

10    On a personal note, I cannot count the number of times I've brought up the continued overrepresentation of whiteness and maleness in the anarchist milieu, particularly in publishing and movements, and been confronted with Emma Goldman as an indication of how that isn't true.

11    For instance, though she did discuss the failure of her comrades to take some aspects of her work seriously, a significant amount of Emma Goldman's writing about misogyny was often a critique of dominant social and political denunciations of sex work and sexuality. In this way, her commentary was often focused on mainstream society rather than explicitly on critiquing anarchist communities.

12    Peggy Kornegger, "Anarchism: The Feminist Connection" in Dark Star Collective, eds. *Quiet Rumors: An Anarcha-Feminist Reader*. 3rd ed. (Oakland: AK Press., 2012), 25–35.

13    See Lynn Farrow's, "Feminism as Anarchism" and Marian Leighton's "Anarcho-Feminism and Louise Michel." in *Quiet Rumors: An Anarcha-Feminist* Reader. 3rd ed. (Oakland: AK Press, 2012).

14    See Nancy Hartsock, *Money, Sex, and Power: Towards a Feminist Historical Materialism*. (Boston: Northeastern University Press, 1985).

15    Peggy Kornegger, "Anarchism: Feminisms Make the Connection" in *Quiet Rumors*, p. 31.

16    Abbey Volcano, and J. Rogue. 2012. "Insurrection at the Intersection: Feminism, Intersectionality, and Anarchism" in *Quiet Rumors*, p. 45.

17    For descriptions and critiques of trans-exclusive radical feminism, see: Julia Serrano. *Excluded: Making Feminist and Queer Movements More Exclusive*. (New York: Seal Press, 2013).

18    This reflects a broader lack of engagement with the question of settler colonialism in anarchist writing and activism. Native feminists have not only developed critiques of capitalism, the state, white supremacy, and heteropatriarchy alongside engagements

with settler colonialism, but have continually emphasized how these critiques are grounded in Native cosmologies rather than influence from the radical Left. What is more, they emphasize the need to disrupt the conflation of indigenous nationalisms and nationalisms that stem from the nation-state.

19    According to the Rape and Incest National Network (RAINN), who draw their statistics from the US Department of Justice, 52% of those arrested for forcible rape were white and between 93% and 98% of those arrested for forcible rape are men. According to the National Transgender Discrimination Survey, 64% of transgender people report being sexual assaulted in their lifetimes. Keep in mind, of course, that these numbers only take into account *reported* instances of sexual assault. Given that sexual assault is one of the least reported violent crimes, it is probable that these rates are much higher.

20    Genealogies and collections of anarchist theory are still predominantly white and male, as one can see through just a cursory glance at the titles published about anarchism in the past 20 years. Though this is slowly changing, there is a long way to go before this balance is shifted to a more equitable representation.

21    Rachel E. Luft, "Looking for Common Ground: Relief Work in Post-Katrina New Orleans as an American Parable of Race and Gender Violence" in *NWSA Journal*, Vol. 20, No. 3, *New Orleans: A Special Issue on Gender, the Meaning of Place, and the Politics of Displacement*, Fall 2008, 5–31.

22    Courtney Desiree Morris, "Why Misogynists Make Great Informants: How Gender Violence on the Left Enables State Violence in Radical Movements." *make/shift: feminisms in motion journal*. Los Angeles, 2010.

23    bell hooks, and Greg Yancy, "bell hooks: Buddhism, the Beats, and Loving Blackness," *The New York Times*, December 10 2015, paragraph 6.

## ABOUT THE AUTHOR

*Theresa is a past recipient of an IAS writing grant.*

*Theresa Warburton lives on Lummi/Coast Salish territory in Bellingham, WA where she teaches US Multiethnic and Native literatures as well as Women's, Gender, and Sexuality Studies. She has been involved in a number of community projects that focus on indigenous sovereignty, reproductive freedom, prisoner support and prison abolition, and working towards new models of addressing sexual and domestic violence. Both her organizing and intellectual work focus on exploring how better attending to the literary interventions stemming from indigenous sovereignty and US/Third World feminist movements can help to realize the radical potential of anarchism in the contemporary moment. She has big dreams but small hands, so is always looking for people with whom to build.*

Art by N.O. Bonzo

everything's better
when we're smashing
together

# INDIGENIST INTERSECTIONALITY:

## DECOLONIZING AND REWEAVING AN INDIGENOUS ECO-QUEER FEMINISM AND ANARCHISM

---

### LAURA HALL

The violence enacted against Indigenous women and Two-Spirit/LGBTQ people evokes deep questions about the intent and impact of colonization in a Canadian settler and state context. The horrors of colonial violence—bodies were violated and abandoned at the sides of highways, in ditches, in rivers—tell stories of the vital importance of Indigenous women's leadership, their warriorhood, their gifts, and their medicines, and also of the centrality of gendered freedom and fluid belonging in Indigenous cultures. It is a system of colonization that seeks to erase and subsume these realities and to replace Indigenous truth with illusions of our weakness. We are at a pivotal moment now as state and settler voices seek to understand what is needed, and it is a pivotal moment best informed by threads of anarchist and feminist thought woven within Indigenous worldviews. Vital intersections are made between gender and Indigeneity because the conversation is always in danger of being rerouted by policing and state voices, as well as settler voices.[1] The work that Indigenous women and Two-Spirit/LGBTQ people do on the ground—to renew our connections to culture, to renew the innovations and economies of our nations—needs more support in every way from allies across intellectual lines.

Much of my organizing work is done with Indigenous women and particularly Two-Spirit/LGBTQ women. The Seven Directions Education Centre is an initiative I started with friends in order

Art by Lesly Yobany Mendoza | justseeds.org

to create space particularly for Indigenous women to work together on cultural renewal and land-based healing and education. I'm often amazed by the ways our group expands on family, in connection with our original families. Through co-creation of a land-based education project, Seven Directions is linking the ways that original economies and food security combine with women's governance and the breaking down of colonial boundaries. We grow gardens with original seeds of our various Indigenous nations, we tap maple trees, and put tobacco down in gratitude for the maple water we take that aids our wellbeing every spring. In the early summer of 2015 when the corn was planted, our group's youngest member walked along the mounds barefoot while her mother and auntie helped her. I could feel the impact of this little girl's communication with Creation. I felt a commitment all over again to the original foods and seeds, the healing of soil and water in partnership with the healing of our bodies, spirits, and minds.

Seven Directions was inspired by the work of Indigenous women like Winona LaDuke and Katsi Cook, who talk about food security, our connections to environment, to Creation, and our responsibilities. Working in partnership with non-Indigenous allies is a goal for our group, but we are often up against very particular blocks. First, that non-Indigenous allies are so often far more concerned with their own connections to land and place, rather than committed to the land return of Indigenous Peoples. Secondly, that their statements about their commitment to decolonization are not combined with solid action and capacity building for Indigenous Peoples to do our own recovery work. And thirdly, that there is a need to reframe resistance as housing,

health, environment, and culture are all connected. Overall, it isn't enough to claim solidarity with Indigenous women against violence without contributing substantively to the work we are doing to create health and well-being for our communities. Much of this paper is an explanation of those interconnections, and of why supporting Indigenous women's initiatives in a deeper way is so vital.

This is my approach to understanding the project of Indigenous cultural renewal and decolonization as a gendered and ecological undoing of settler colonial society and the colonial state. I turn to Indigenous thinkers, particularly those who map the confines of colonialism as a gendered, sexualized and violent system, one that is intent on using particular kinds of state-centric responses in order to engulf Indigenous societies. Indigenist theories are written about in intersecting ways that necessarily root us in land-based, ecological realities. When the priorities of Indigenous women and Two-Spirit/LGBTQ are centered, and a worldview rooted in Indigenous knowledge comprises our framework, a host of issues can be better approached—including, perhaps most centrally, solutions to violence against Indigenous people—in ways that do not allow police state infrastructure and ideology to infringe on forward movement.

What Taiaiake Alfred calls "anarch@indigenism" is grounded in Indigenous thought,[2] inclusive of gendered fluidity and non-hierarchal community structures within governance systems gifted and understood through Creation stories/truths. As such, I argue that Indigenist feminist and anarchist intersections are vital spaces, particularly at a time when violence against Indigenous women and Indigenous lands has become so central to our concerns, and when renewing the treaty-based and caring relationships becomes so important to our survival and wellbeing. Land and environmental appropriation and destruction are at the foundation of a colonizing system that violates and disappears Indigenous women and Two-Spirit/ LGBTQ people. Indigenist anarchist thought is necessarily gendered as on one hand, the centrality of women's leadership is important in Indigenous contexts, and on the other hand, the fluidity of gender and choices about sexual freedom are rooted in Indigenous worldviews as well. Intersections between Indigenous and anarchist theories can richly inform and effectively address issues facing Indigenous communities who are overseen by state and settler colonialism in many overlapping ways.

## SITUATING SELF

I also name my approach reflective of my own positionality, as Queerness/ Two-Spirit/LGBTQed Indigeneity, and the responsibilities of being a woman in ways I negotiate daily, honoring both women as a group and the fluidity of Indigenous gendering, by actively dismantling the daily realities of heteropatriarchal colonialism. My mother's family, mixed Indigenous-Franco-Canadian on her mother's side, rooted in the Timmins areas and in Kahnawake on her father's side before Residential and Day schooling caused some to disperse, deeply informs my commitment to renewal of culture and return of original territory to Indigenous nations. I am using Two-Spirit/LGBTQ as a label to describe a range of identities that Indigenous people might adopt in the English language. On a personal note, I like the hybridity of the mash-up of concepts, because it reflects my own hybridity. Hybridity in this case is about becoming and learning, from all of my stories, with the intent of explaining why the centrality of women's leadership and women's perspectives does not negate the need to discuss gender fluidity in original Indigenous languages. Hybridity and paradox are embodied and lived experiences as I seek knowledge that is grounded and authentic.

## INDIGENOUS WORLDVIEW

Indigenous Peoples as nations with supra-state status, "as not synonymous with the states that claimed to have subsumed them,"[3] present an alternative vision of governance rooted in treaty that ensures environmental sustainability, gendered equity and fluidity, and non-hierarchal relationships between Indigenous and non-Indigenous Peoples. Creation stories among Indigenous nations explain and root origins and understanding, not as a set of "myths," but as truth embedded in all of Creation.[4] Creation stories tell us about the supreme respect given to women creators, like Sky Woman among the Haudenosaunee, whose lineage gifts women with responsibilities for governance and economic leadership.[5]

Creation, at some point in ancient time, birthed entire peoples with processes for governing themselves through conflict and grand world changes. For the Haudenosaunee, Creation began with Sky Woman and her daughter and grandchildren. Subsequent generations in the line experienced difficulties leading to new ideas and governing structures. The Great Law of Peace is one such example, providing new settler governments with a vision of something more than what they had known. Barbara Alice Mann is among those who point out that it is contemporary generations who have forgotten those original influences of The Great Law on American governments,[6] while Oren Lyons and John Mohawk[7] point out that among the ideas discarded by early Euro-American governments were Haudenosaunee notions of egalitarian gender and class relations, as well as environmental sustainability.

In order to create good relationships with people who were not well socialized in the ways of Indigenous democracies, treaties were made to plant the seeds for ongoing Indigenous freedom and sharing of resources. Indigenous interpretations of treaty relations are vital to understand at a time when settler society searches for alternatives to the state colonial system. In James Sakej Youngblood Henderson's critical analysis of Hobbesian thinking as a justification for colonization, he writes, "[t]he idea of colonization has remained immune to the issues of the law of nature and the treaty commonwealth. This immunity resides in the belief that Indigenous people could not make treaties and flies in the face of evidence that the imperial Crown did make treaties with the Indigenous nations."[8] Indigenous nations and confederacies made treaties with new settlers that continue to form a basis of sustainable and equitable relationships. Centrally, the Kuswentha or Two-Row Wampum is described by Haudenosaunee thinkers in this way, embedding the people in original responsibilities:

The design of this wampum symbolizes a path called the "river of life" where both the Haudenosaunee canoe and the European ship travel. The symbolic paths were intentionally parallel in order to indicate the agreed understanding that neither nation was to interfere in the affairs or governance of the other. The three rows of white wampum between the two paths denote respect, friendship, and trust, three principles that keep the two nations close, but at a respectful distance…The "river of life" is an apt symbol of the nature of treaty relations. While other peoples may view treaties as individual transactions, the Haudenosaunee see them in the context of the relationship they have with the other nation: if the relationship is the river, the treaties are stones that mark spots along its way.[9]

Indigenous treaty relations allow for a continuity of governance, social and economic stability, rooted in an Indigenous worldview rather than colonial relations.

Indigenous people's knowledge systems are particular to their land base and flow from that ecological embeddedness, for example, in Vine Deloria's words,

We have already seen that tribal peoples observed the world around them and quickly concluded that it represented an energetic mind undergirding the physical world… This belief…is the starting point, not the conclusion.[10]

Indigenous governance structures provide also the interconnections between a gendered system of egalitarian relations and environmental rootedness. Under Haudenosaunee law, women have "proprietorship of 'the land and the soil'" as "Turtle Island was created specifically for Sky Woman, whose legal heirs were her direct lineal descendants in the female line." And further, "Haudenosaunee people did, quite literally, spring from the wombs of Sky Woman and the Lynx (her daughter)...It is a literal statement of fact, not 'Indian hyperbole.'"[11]

Identity in relation to Creation, not only to land but to Clans, is also emphasized by Barbara Mann, whose work is immensely important toward understanding the deeper implications of Indigenism and gendering. These are the original governance systems, rooted in respect and equity for all of life. Paying lip service to equality within a state-colonial system that is inherently heterosexist and patriarchal, is counter- productive but also a distraction from the renewal of Indigenous governance systems. For example,

> [A]ccording to the Blackfoot (Siikisikaawa), governance is not limited to soyipihtsiiksi (the person who is of, and speaks for the people) or the nonauthoritative, nonhierarchical and noncoercive relations between people. Governance exists as a relationship with the "circle of life" or all beings within a territory, and it is about people establishing a relationship with a territory and learning from that relationship.[12]

Haudenosaunee scholars have long made the link between the environmental degradation associated with industrial overdevelopment, the undermining of land and water rights, and the need to return to original teachings that ground Indigenous rights and responsibilities. As Hill writes:

> Our historical consciousness, our land and our environmental ethics are inextricably connected. For the Haudenosaunee, history on this earth begins with Creation. The Haudenosaunee creation story is a

detailed epic taking days to tell in its entirety. Additional side stories relate to the time of Creation and help explain how other entities of this world came into being.[13]

Creation is Indigenous truth and reality unfolding. Creation is not myth or metaphor or constructed reality. Creation truths inform Indigenous worldview while Eurocentric infringement continually seeks to deny Creation in order to justify settler society's rights to alter economies, restructure land relations, and create a whole system of colonial protectionism to the total detriment and continual undoing of Indigenous responsibilities and rights.

In Katsi Cook's words, women are the "first environment"[14] and Indigenous women are harmed by the toxification of the water, in health and physical embodiment of that direct and intentional harm, and also as leaders and keepers of the water, in the sense that a whole governance system, familial organization, and community wellbeing are equally undone. There is no saving of environments without looking to the root causes of the environment's undoing, and there is no addressing of Indigenous self-determination without environmental wellbeing as equally central. That there are direct physical, spiritual, and intellectual connections between Indigenous women and the land and water, is evident across many cultural teachings. Joe Sheridan and Roronhiakewen Dan Longboat explain the knowledge base of Indigenous cultures as inherently rooted in original ecologies. Human beings in an ecological context

> ...are sacred teachers meant to impart and remember and are duty bound to the spiritual because we were the last beings created. The

other creatures chose, as part of their responsibilities, the duty of caring for us and also exercised their spiritual and intellectual capabilities by instilling in us and sharing among us their knowledge of how to live, their stories, songs, and identities.[15]

Indigenist-feminist and Two-Spirit/LGBTQ people focus on important state challenges, building on Indigenist-anarchist theory and repositioning Indigenous knowledge at the center of revolutionary action and thought. The primary challenge within this work might lie with the simple reminder that for decolonization to be realized, gendered resistance to colonial state systems necessitates the centering of Indigenous Peoples' issues, perspectives and priorities. At the same time this is an intersectional framework fully recognizing the dynamic and growing nature of Indigenous resistance and culture-based renewal as Indigenous Peoples weed out and heal from the damages of colonial impositions. I argue elsewhere that the violent and coercive undoing of Indigenous women's economies has remained central to the Canadian colonial state and settler colonial project since its beginnings.[16] This is the focus, the point of intersection, that begs us to look away from colonial solutions to colonial problems, and to stop pathologizing and blaming Indigenous Peoples for choices made in a context of ongoing colonization and land loss. Indigenist anarchist interventions contribute an understanding that intensified state and settler framing, policing and legalization of the issues and challenges facing Indigenous Peoples in a colonial era, actively reinforces ongoing fracturing and oppression.

A vision of Indigenistanarchism is provided by Taiaiake Alfred in visioning for a return of Indigenous Peoples "to a place of dignity and strength and in repossession of our homelands, governed by our own laws, and recentered as human beings guided by the Original Teachings of our ancestors about how to live in peace together and in relation to the natural environment" while newcomers, including anarchist thinkers, "appreciate the justice of this vision and...live humbly as a guest according to Indigenous North American laws."[17]

Sheridan and Longboat talk through the significance of understanding that Indigenous thought comes from the land, not as symbolic invention of human intellect, but as direct communication. They write of the spiritual centeredness of life,

Spiritual force is the timeless heartbeat of Indigeneity. It preserves a human identity that is symmetrical with traditional territory, while acting as a protection from environmental conceptions and practices that diminish and exclude the Ancestors and spirit beings that travel the universe in the spiritual realms of the temporal and spatial dimensions that belong to them.[18]

The centrality of Indigenous women's scholarship to the work of decolonization and cultural revitalization cannot be over-emphasized. Indeed, the vital importance of Indigenous women's leadership in feminist movements in the West is often obscured by Eurocentric scholarship.[19] I remain inspired by the work of Indigenous women like Trish Monture and Laara Fitznor. Fitznor writes about "storying" as an active rooting of knowledge in identity and experience.[20] Monture's seminal *Thunder in My Soul* contains the description of an Indigenist situated knowledge, where she writes, "It is only through my culture that my women's identity is shaped. It is the teachings of my people that demand we speak from our own personal experience."[21] Resistance is rooted in fluid, ever growing, ever creative cultural traditions.

## SETTLER AND STATE COLONIALISM

Interrupting Indigenous governance and sustainable livelihoods is a complex system of colonialism in need of study from within. Indigenist anarchist, feminist, and Two-Spirit/LGBTQ thinkers hold space for vital discussion about the gendered and hierarchal nature of the colonial system. The deliberateness of poverty and restructured economies as a weapon against Indigenous women's leadership and the deliberate architecture of heteropatriarchal family structures and community hierarchies combine with the perpetuation of the violability of Indigenous bodies, particularly those of Indigenous women and Two-Spirit/LGBTQ people; the most vulnerable in communities coping with high rates of addiction and violence are "inherently violable."[22] Addressing the nature of heterosexism and misogyny, or "heteropatriarchy" remains central to decolonization efforts.[23] This work continues to be rooted in the whole cultural and environmental context of Indigenous knowledge. Walters and Simoni write about the rootedness of Indigenous women's leadership, in Creation stories that also root Indigenous nations in particular places, adhering to and learning from, particular spirits of place. And so,

Spiritual female figures reflect the sacred and central positions that women have held among indigenous nations over many centuries. Contemporarily, Native women's power is manifested in their roles as sacred life givers, teachers, socializers of children, healers, doctors, seers, and warriors. With their status in these powerful roles, Native women have formed the core of indigenous resistance to colonization, and the health of their communities in many ways depends upon them.[24]

Estrada writes about Two-Spirit/LGBTQ identity, translating *Niizh Manitoag* from the Algonquin language group, as the origin of Two-Spirit as a concept of a non-binaried gendered Creator.[24] Among Haudenosaunee, sexual freedom is discussed as a component of matrilineal society.[25]

Advocates for the rights of Indigenous women and Two-Spirit/LGBTQ people provide a rooted intersectional approach. As Colleen Hele, Naomi Sayers and Jessica Wood write,

...many Indigenous organizations will be quick to treat the Sixties Scoop and violence against Indigenous women and girls as separate issues — thereby ignoring the history of state-sanctioned trafficking of Indigenous children and ongoing colonial policies that continue to create violence in the lives of Indigenous women, girls and Two-Spirit/LGBTQ people. These same organizations will also be quick to point to prostitution as the sole problem that permits human trafficking to take place, instead of examining, for example, how the lack of safe and adequate housing in our communities pushes Indigenous women and girls into unsafe situations.[26]

Indigenist feminism should challenge the interferences of policing and state entities in the lives of Indigenous women by contextualizing the violence that Indigenous women face as an issue of state and settler colonialism. Indigenist feminism not only centers the reclamation of land and culture as an inherently anti-patriarchal project, but challenges non-Indigenous feminist movements to challenge the state and settler focus of anti-sexist work. Jason Michael Adams intersects anarchist, Indigenist and feminist theory in order to map the unique positionality of Indigenous women: as they are subjected to

...practices of sterilization and a culture of rape, Indigenous women are "biologized" - they are rendered as "internal enemies," objects of state domestication, administration and eradication. Both "present," in order to be rendered governable subjects and "absent" in order to render the founding violence of the nation-state imperceptible, Native American women are reduced to the precarious status of bare life, forced to perform these nuances of "present absence" as the situation requires.[27]

The subsuming of Indigenous women's presence and status is the removal of their power in tribal contexts. In other words, it is the colonial removal of leaders of the highest order. Hoping that colonial thinkers are simply too naïve and unaware of women's power and influence to enact such deliberate undermining, seems dangerous. The deliberateness and destructiveness of the colonial system is a purposeful tide of violence and violation.

The system is contextualized by colonial land relations, whereby settler society is encouraged to erase Indigenous governance and Indigenous bodies, and the state provides impetus and inspiration to continue the project of land expropriation and destruction. Tuck and Yang describe settler colonialism in terms of its replication in myriad systems and theories that seek to justify the expropriation of Indigenous lands and cultures for the use of settler society and the settler state. It is only through the "repatriation of Indigenous land and life," as Tuck and Yang remind us, that those systems of power are truly "unsettled."[28] The potential for coming together lies not in pushing Indigenous knowledge(s) to fit within Eurocentric settler-colonial priorities, but in dismantling the rootedness of domination. As the authors continue, "The metaphorization of decolonization makes possible a set of evasions, or 'settler moves to innocence,' that problematically attempt to reconcile settler guilt and complicity, and rescue settler futurity."[29]

A political movement that fails to understand colonialism's centrality to daily life in the Americas is destined, it would seem, to perpetuate its dynamics. For example, vital questions were raised during Occupy movements in 2011 about economic inequality and poverty, and the ability of individuals to build community not hindered by state oppression.[30] Intersections between Occupy and Indigenous, feminist, and anti-imperial movements were raised immediately. Barker points out the irony in the use of the term "occupy" on already occupied Indigenous lands:

Long before the goal of settler colonialism was clearly articulated—the transfer of all land from Indigenous to Settler control; the erasure and replacement of Indigenous space with settler colonial spaces; the naturalization of Settler people on the land— Indigenous activists understood this inevitable trajectory and began moving to check it.[31]

Settler colonialism continues to block social justice movements from finding solutions to the issues they face. Govier writes, "patterns of colonization, land use, racism, disregard for treaties, and the residential school system: we are linked significantly to the institutions that are responsible," meaning that non-Indigenous Canadians "are beneficiaries of the injustices."[32] The argument follows then that rectifying the entitlements of colonialism would actually benefit social and economic justice movements. As Tuck and Yang argue, there is potential in what is "incommensurable" between Indigenous and Western knowledge systems.[33] Treaty-based resistance movements are named as emancipatory theory whereby allies become accomplices in the dismantling of the damages of colonization.

There are moments of convergence between anarchist and Indigenous scholars, but as Barker and Pickerill point out, tensions caused by settler appropriation and misapprehension of Indigenous priorities are too common.[34] The Occupy movement is an example of the authors' concerns about settler missteps in relation to Indigenous land-based politics. The point that I am raising is that these are also deeply gendered contestations, not only as spatial relationality, but as temporal belonging rooted in Creation and forever-belonging.[35]

## GENDERING THE CONVERSATION

There is a need for more Two-Spirit/LGBTQ focus in gendered discussions about the freedom and emancipation of Indigenous Peoples. We need support, time, and space, to renew language and cultural understandings of women's sacredness and leadership and gender fluidity as manifest in each culture. Other important issues arise when heterosexist patriarchal colonialism is challenged, about how centrally positive sexuality, pleasure, and freedom are rooted within Indigenous traditions. It remains important to provide these critiques; it is not said often enough that Indigenous traditions are flexible and able to explain the responsibilities and belonging of Two-Spirit/LGBTQ community members. It is this articulation of responsibilities that theorists like Cameron ask of the holders of Indigenous culture.

Native women and Native Two Spirit, transgender, and gender nonconforming people are subjected to gender-specific forms of law enforcement violence, such as racial profiling, physical abuse, sexual harassment and abuse, and failure to respond or abusive responses to reports of violence.... Native women are also profiled as drug users, alcohol abusers, and as bad mothers.[36]

Indigenist feminist theory would also look at the ways that Indigenous bodies and economies of pleasure are affected by colonialism.

Examples of the colonial intersection of land- and gender-based oppression come in many forms. Gendered and environmental violence work together in a colonial system. For example, Indigenous activists combine an anarchist critique of state and policing entities in the lives of Indigenous women, with the centering of women's voices in discourses that most concern them. Some of the most important work happening in Indigenous scholarship is cer.:ered on the resistance efforts and priorities of Indigenous women and Two-Spirit/LGBTQ people who engage in sex work. Sayers and Hunt write about "the importance of supporting indigenous women where they're at today regardless of the choices they make and the utility of community-based initiatives to increase safety and wellness for all," and continue that

> We see that even in the midst of poverty, abuse, and marginalization, native women's daily decisions need to be respected, and the lives of those women choosing to sell sex are as valuable as those choosing to work for government agencies. Violence against all native women needs to be made unacceptable, including against those who work in the sex trade.[37]

Sayers and Hunt's words also speak to deep reflection about the roots of Indigenous governance. The leadership of Indigenous women and Two-Spirit/LGBTQ people is evoked. Addressing violence against Indigenous women is central to dismantling settler and state colonial systems.

Ongoing resistance efforts attempt to grapple with state interference and reframing at every turn. In 2010, The Native Women's Association of Canada's Sisters in Spirit initiative released their report on the growing numbers of Indigenous women who are murdered or disappeared in the Canadian settler state matrix. The state's response to Sisters in Spirit was to cease their funding, and to divert funds to a Royal Canadian Mounted Police database,[38] raising important questions about Indigenous community control over policing, and the overseeing of Indigenous communities by state policing and prison systems. In Amnesty International's words,

> Resource allocation and programming to tackle this violence and its root causes have been piecemeal and without a guiding strategy or coordination. Although in 2010 the federal government announced plans to spend $10 million over five years to address violence against Indigenous women and girls, most of the funding was earmarked for police initiatives that track missing persons in general, without any particular focus on the specific patterns of gender-based violence against Indigenous women and girls. Furthermore, organizations working to advance the rights of Indigenous women and girls and address issues of violence, such as the Native Women's Association of Canada, continue to face an uncertain funding climate.[39]

This redirection revealed important intersections between gender and colonization, both in terms of the state's willingness to appropriate the conversation for its own purposes, and in terms of the centrality of gender-based oppression to the broad project of settler and state colonialism. Indeed, the spatial or place-based as well as temporal parameters (defined in terms of deep time and belonging in the Americas) of Indigenous thought and practice necessitate a gendered approach that seeks to recenter a diversity of Indigenous voices.[40] Indigenist anarchist, feminist, and Two-Spirit/ LGBTQ analyses all have the potential to recreate those pathways of renewal within Indigenous thinking, revealing tactics of state and settler colonialism.

Indigenist feminist, anarchist, and Two-Spirit/LGBTQ intersections are especially illuminating at a time when LGBT mainstream politics has become ingrained in a hegemonic state system, prioritizing state-sanctioned marriage and a kind of emergent nationalist discourse. Indigenous Two-Spirit/LGBTQ interventions decenter LGBT politics from what has become an integrationist and heteropatriarchal nationalist project. Rankin iterates an analysis of Canadian nation-building as intrinsically heteropatriarchal and heterosexist, and points out that discussion about same-sex marriage and integrating LGBT politics in the nation-state take place "within an era in which the masculinist character of contemporary Canadian nationalism appears to be deepening."[4] This is, in essence, a non-patriarchal nationalism, which Rankin's work also mentions in passing, as a point of interest that should be expanded upon by Two-Spirit/LGBTQ/ Indigenist feminist scholars. Gendering the work of decolonization is about renewing original governance systems, inclusive of family and communities that embody principles of egalitarian and caring traditions.

Weaving theories in this way can keep conversation flowing away from the state-centric legislative approach that sees collective rights pitted against individual rights, toward a deeper reclamation of Indigenist feminist principles in practice, rooted as they are in Indigenous knowledge and traditions. The implications of this kind of work are far-reaching, basically requiring a recentering of Indigenous and Two-Spirit politics.

Indigenist intersectionality as a Two-Spirit project is a reclamation of identity as emerging into community, to full inclusion. It is a critique of heteropatriarchal influences on Indigenous nationhood, and therefore a reclamation of older matrilineal traditions.

Indigenist intersectional theory allows us to embody an ethic of freedom, choice, responsibility, and thanksgiving. This is a project of renewing healthy relationships within individuals, with each other, and with the land, central to treaty relations. Considering the ways that sexual violence has been used by colonizing society to fracture and harm individuals and families, the reclaiming of sexual freedom, and of consenting, caring relationships, is vital. At the same time, the dominance of heteropatriarchal mores necessitates deeper questions about gender and sexuality in Indigenous contexts. The conversation is growing, like seeds buried, and is expansive rather than limiting.

The implications of these interconnections mean that Indigenous scholarship can continue to grow its capacity as a deeply gendered, environmentally sustainable project. It also means that social and environmental justice is impossible in the Americas without the leadership of Indigenous women, knowledge keepers, elders, youth, and all members of communities dispersed by ongoing colonialism. Progressive movements for change in the Americas, inclusive of anarchist and feminist movements, cannot tokenize or marginalize Indigenous Peoples if they are to find success in their aims.

Intersecting an analysis of the gendered, ecological and supra state status of Indigenous nations, means understanding and supporting those who challenge the state's latest strategies in an unending wave of liberal/conservative shifts and austerity/abundance funding structures which consistently fails to challenge the nature of settler state colonialism. In the (supposedly) post-austerity, post-conservative, post-Harper shift to a Liberal government, signs of the need for expansive and re-rooted decolonizing thought—a renewal once again of the very thinking that led to Idle No More and other movements to resist Harper's efforts at undoing treaty relationships—were apparent from the start. Indigenous Peoples, original to and preceding the nation-state, were pressured on social media to support settler efforts to vote Harper out. An Inquiry into the root causes of extreme violence against Indigenous women almost immediately excluded family of an extended, non-hetero/biological kind, and the families who were included seemed to be rushed toward exposing their heartache and grief and pain for speedy bureaucrats. We are still far from admitting that colonialism is rooted in a pathology of white supremacist, heterosexist, patriarchal violence, and that the bad medicines unleashed by ongoing attempts at absorbing, assimilating, and eradicating Indigenous Peoples and nationhood are with us still. There is danger in appealing to a state responsible for violence against Indigenous women, and in erasing the real roots of that violence among policing, corporate and social bodies.

## NOTES

1    Sarah Hunt, "Why Are We Hesitant to Name White Male Violence as a Root Cause," Rabble News (September 2014).

2    Taiaiake Alfred, Wasase: Indigenous Pathways of Action and Freedom (Peterborough, Ont.: Broadview Press, 2005).

3    Dian Million, Therapeutic Nations: Healing in an Age of Indigenous Human Rights (Tucson: University of Arizona Press, 2013), 13.

4    Joe Sheridan and Roronhiakewen 'He Clears the Sky' Dan Longboat, "Walking Back Into Creation: Environmental Apartheid and the Eternal—Initiating an Indigenous Mind Claim," Space and Culture 17:3 (2014), 308-324.

5    Barbara Alice Mann, Iroquoian Women: The Gantowisas (New York: Peter Lang, 2000).

6    Bruce E. Johansen, Debating Democracy: Native American Legacy of Freedom (Santa Fe: Clear Light Books, 1998).

7    Curtis Berkey, Donald A. Grinde., Oren Lyons, et al., Exiled in the Land of the Free: Democracy, Indian Nations, and the U.S. Constitution (Santa Fe: Clear Light Books, 1992).

8    James Sakej Youngblood Henderson, The Context of the State of Nature: Reclaiming Indigenous Voice and Vision (Victoria: UBC Press, 2000), 27.

9    Brenda E. LaFrance and James E. Costello, "The Haudenosaunee Environmental Protection Process (HEPP): Reinforcing the Three Principles of Goodmindedness, Peacefulness, and Strength to Protect the Natural World," Preserving Tradition and Understanding the Past: Papers from the Conference on Iroquois Research, 2001-2005, 63-64.

10    Vine Deloria Jr., The World We Used To Live In (Golden, CO: Fulcrum Publishing, 2006), 197.

11    Barbara A. Mann, "The Lynx in Time: Haudenosaunee Women's Traditions and History," American Indian Quarterly 21:3 (1997), 424.

12    Kiera Ladner, "Governing Within an Ecological Context: Creating an AlterNative Understanding of Blackfoot Governance," Studies in Political Economy 70 (2003), 125.

13    Susan Hill, "'Travelling Down the River of Life Together in Peace and Friendship, Forever': Haudenosaunee Land Ethics and Treaty Agreements as the Basis For Restructuring the Relationship with the British Crown," in Leanne Simpson, ed., Lighting the Eighth Fire (Winnipeg: Arbeiter Ring, 2008), 24.

14    Katsi Cook," Women are the First Environment," Indian Country (December 23, 2003).

15    Sheridan and Longboat, "Walking Back Into Creation," 308.

16    Hill, "Travelling Down the River," 24.

17    Alfred, Wasase, 4.

18    Sheridan and Longboat, "Walking Back Into Creation," 309.

19    Mann, "The Lynx in Time," 424.

20    Joy Hendry and Laara Fitznor, *Anthropologists, Indigenous Scholars and the Research Endeavour: Seeking Bridges Toward Mutual Respect* (Abingdon: Taylor And Francis, 2012), 270, 281.

21    P. Monture-Angus, *Thunder in My Soul: A Mohawk Woman Speaks* (Halifax: Fernwood Publishing, 1995), 29

22    Andrea Smith, "Unmasking the State: Racial/Gender Terror and Hate Crimes," *Australian Feminist Law Journal* 26 (2007).

23    Andrea Smith, "Heteropatriarchy and the Three Pillars of White Supremacy: Rethinking Women of Color Organizing," in *The Color of Violence: The Incite! Anthology* (Brooklyn: South End Press, 2006).

24    K. Walters and J. Simoni, "Reconceptualizing Native Women's Health: An 'Indigenist' Stress-Coping Model," *American Journal of Public Health* 92:4 (2002), 520.

25    Mann, "The Lynx in Time," 424.

26 Colleen Hele, Naomi Sayers, and Jessica Wood, "What's Missing from the Conversation on Missing and Murdered Indigenous Women and Girls," *The Toast*, September 14, 2015.

27    Jason Michael Adams, "'Only a Stranger at Home: Urban Indigeneity and the Ontopolitics of International Relations," *Affinities: A Journal of Radical Theory, Culture, and Action* 5:1 (2011).

28    Eve Tuck and K. Wayne Yang, "Decolonizing is Not a Metaphor," *Decolonization: Indigeneity, Education & Society*, 1, 1 (2012), 1.

29    Tuck and Yang, "Decolonizing is Not a Metaphor," 1.

31    Adam J. Barker, "Already Occupied: Indigenous Peoples, Settler Colonialism and the Occupy Movements in North America," *Social Movement Studies: Journal of Social, Cultural and Political Protest*, 11, 3-4 (2012). 332.

32    Govier (2010), 35.

33    Tuck and Yang, "Decolonizing is Not a Metaphor," 1.

34    Adam J. Barker and Jenny Pickerill, "Radicalizing Relationships To and Through Shared Geographies: Why Anarchists Need to Understand Indigenous Connections to Land and Place," *Antipode*, 44:5 (November, 2012), 1-2.

35    Sheridan and Longboat, *Walking Back Into Creation*," 309.

36    Incite! "Law Enforcement Violence Against Native Women, Native Trans People, & Two Spirit People." Incite-national.org, 2014.

37    Naomi Sayers and Sarah Hunt, "Abolition of Sex Work Won't End Violence Against Native Women," *The Globe and Mail*, January 22, 2015.

38    D. Beeby, "RCMP Database on Missing Persons is Overdue, Over Budget," *CBC News*, August 31, 2015.

39    Amnesty International (2014), 4.

40    Sheridan and Longboat, Walking Back Into Creation," 309.

41    L. Pauline Rankin, ""Sexualities and National Identities: Re-imagining Queer Nationalism." Journal of Canadian Studies 35:2 (Summer 2000), 176.

## ABOUT THE AUTHOR

*Laura received an IAS writing grant to complete this essay.*

*Laura Hall is thankful to be part of a family with Haudenosaunee (Kanienkehaka) and British roots. Having grown up and learned on Anishinaabe territory in Northern Ontario, the author is also immensely grateful for the Elders and Knowledge Keepers who remind us that radical and revolutionary thought is rooted in an Indigenous worldview and in the land. Laura is currently completing a PhD in Environmental Studies at York University, with an emphasis on Haudenosaunee community planning. Her work utilizes a decolonizing intersectional lens that necessarily prioritizes and centers the concerns of Indigenous Peoples, inclusive of the return of their lands and full cultural autonomy.*

# THOUGHTS ON AN ANARCHIST RESPONSE TO HEPATITIS C AND HIV

## ZOË DODD AND ALEXANDER McLELLAND

"As a woman living with HIV, I am often asked whether there will ever be a cure for AIDS. My answer is that there is already a cure. It lies in the strength of women, families and communities, who support and empower each other to break the silence around HIV/AIDS and take control…"
—Beatrice Were Ugandan AIDS activist[1]

In the early days of the HIV epidemic, within a context of massive and systemic state neglect, people came together out of desperation and urgency to help care for and support their own communities, friends, and families. Some helped people die with dignity in non-stigmatizing environments, while others pooled and distributed medications in buyers' clubs. Still others established collective community clinics and organizations for prevention, support, and care. Some distributed sterile equipment for injecting drugs or opened supervised consumption sites without official institutional approval. Despite these productive examples, the devastating past of the AIDS crisis is not one to be romanticized. In looking back at history, these radical actions were inherently anarchist, though at the time people's intentions may not have been rooted in an anarchist worldview. People

Art by Aaron Hughes/Combat Paper/
Steve Lambert

survived despite what authorities deemed appropriate. These examples demonstrate mutual aid, spontaneity, trust, and collaboration—all tenets of anarchism.

In the early days of AIDS organizing there was an anarchist component to New York City's AIDS Coalition To Unleash Power (ACT UP), Toronto's AIDS ACTION NOW!, and there have been many smaller anarchist AIDS activist initiatives over the years. This project aims to reconnect these past movements to what is happening or could happen today.

We have decades of experience with Hepatitis C and HIV as radicals, anarchists, activists, researchers, and frontline workers. Born out of frustration and a desire to create change, our project is aimed to examine with an anarchist worldview ways of thinking by those most impacted by Hepatitis C and/or HIV, and to merge these ideas to put health into their own hands. We are undertaking an ongoing writing project to make links between healthcare responses and anarchist principles.[2] Discussions with activists, workers, anarchists, and people living with Hepatitis C and/or HIV in Canada have informed this project.

We examine the capitalist organization of healthcare, reactive forms of community-based politics, and interventions focused on homogenization and hierarchical intervention, often top-down projects of prescription and standardization. The capitalist organization of health care and the reactive position of activists in the HIV and Hepatitis C community have been limited by funding bodies, disciplinary forms of knowledge, or what is able to be marketized. We seek to stretch the imaginations of HIV and Hepatitis C responses beyond the current prevailing reality.

We have the tools to save lives, but instead, society is organized to allow for the deaths of millions of people. Through our larger writing project, we rethink our current system's response to HIV and Hepatitis C while simultaneously imagining models of collective organizing.

We have chosen to focus this article and our ongoing writing project on HIV and Hepatitis C because of our work and personal connections to these epidemics. We also highlight their shared elements; both HIV and Hepatitis C are highly stigmatized diseases that disproportionately impact marginalized and state-neglected communities, and both emerged under neo-liberalism.

## THE CAPITALIST ORGANIZATION OF HEALTHCARE

"The worst enemy of a government is its own population"
—Noam Chomsky, linguist and anarchist[3]

We are currently thirty years into the HIV crisis and over twenty years into the Hepatitis C epidemic, the first major globalized health epidemics to emerge under the neoliberal world order. Globally, 350,000 to 500,000 deaths are attributed to Hepatitis C and over one million deaths due to AIDS-related causes every year.[4] This primarily impacts the world's most marginalized peoples: the poor, people who use drugs, women, people in prison, people of color, gay and bisexual men, trans people, sex workers, and young people.

As a distinct form of capitalist political and social organization, neo-liberalism came about in the mid-1970s and has been focused on cutting back social programs, on individualism, entrepreneurship, a reduction of the state, privatization, corporate and managerial rationality, and efficiency through competition. The managerial logic of neoliberalism organizes our capitalist system of healthcare, intertwined with profit-driven transnational corporations. Illness is now profitable. The ways we respond to HIV and Hepatitis C are prescribed by top-down institutions with the aim of making or saving money. In this system, there have been massive biomedical advances, billions of dollars "invested" in biomedical research, thousands of non-governmental organizations, public-private partnerships, billion-dollar marketing campaigns, and multiple multimillion-dollar touring conferences.

Using the managerial language and logic of the corporate sector, this professionalized global HIV and Hepatitis C response limits what is possible, including framing how knowledge and meaning are produced. Positivist, measurable, quantifiable and "expert" forms of knowledge provide a professional image that is both efficient and strategic within capitalism. Social science research on HIV and Hepatitis C often reveals what people on the ground already know. "Expert knowledge," as a commodity, justifies hierarchical decision-making and loses sight of people's actual needs. Such is the case when creating "evidence" on the benefits of housing for people living with HIV and Hepatitis C. There is even an annual tour and conference on housing and HIV. Randomized control trials are done for housing of active drug users, linked to care, managed in close contact with the police as a method to reduce HIV infections. Resources are diverted to expertized research, instead of affordable housing.[5]

While there is no cure for HIV, since the mid-1990s, drugs can effectively block the virus from replicating, suppressing HIV. People can live with the virus for their natural lives while no longer being infectious. These drugs save people's lives–but only for those who have access. The system privileges pharmaceutical company patents and profit, further exacerbating global wealth disparities. Medications are still out of reach for fifteen million people.

For Hepatitis C, new treatments have shown cure rates of 90 to 100 percent with limited side effects. Gilead Pharmaceuticals stands to earn $30 billion by 2020 from their new Hepatitis C treatment.[6] The drugs currently cost $1,000 USD per pill per day, for a course of treatment costing a total of $84,000.[7] Yet, the cost to manufacture is less than $250 for the full course of treatment.[8] While society now can effectively cure Hepatitis C, this drug is still out of reach for many. Access to these treatments is extremely limited, and people are dying.

### THE PROBLEM OF DEFENSIVE FORMS OF ACTIVIST STRUGGLE

Projects on Hepatitis C and HIV often focus on defensive struggles to respond to and document the violence of governments and state institutions. Those projects identify bureaucratic and legal barriers to treatment and care, or highlight regressive laws criminalizing drug users, sex workers, and people living with HIV and/or Hepatitis C. The community organizing around Hepatitis C and HIV makes claims on the state, including claims for human rights, funding, and entitlements for forms of citizenship. This results in activists and community groups working to address administrative, institutional, bureaucratic, and legal barriers imposed by higher authorities, while reinforcing the role of the authorities. Community-based organizations are put into tenuous relationships with the authorities who provide funding for HIV and Hepatitis C programs.

Groups clamour to document or reveal the latest ways "key populations" (such as sex workers, people who use drugs, gay men and other men who have sex with men) are marginalized or barred access to rights of health and citizenship to develop "new" evidence. The disastrous conservative policy or intervention becomes the newest research topic to dissect, consume, critique, and produce knowledge.

Some defensive activist struggles include the opposition to the war on people who use drugs. For people who use drugs, the rising rate of new infections of HIV and Hepatitis C can be attributed to criminalization, targeting and incarcerating millions. The war on drugs denies access to autonomy to reduce infections through harm reduction interventions, like needle distribution, supervised consumption sites, and opioid substitution therapy. Doctors can deny those with drug use history access to treatment. Although in the guidelines for Hepatitis C treatment in Canada drug use does not preclude treatment, professionals can deny treatment based on moral judgments about prior drug use. Although in Canada people who inject drugs make up 70 percent of new infections, only about 1 percent have received treatment.[9]

Other defensive struggles include resistance to the criminalization of HIV exposure and non-disclosure (not telling sex partners that one is HIV-positive). Canada criminalizes people with HIV who do not tell partners their HIV status, with one 185 cases brought before the courts as of this writing.[10] The most

frequent charge is aggravated sexual assault, one of the harshest in the Canadian Criminal Code. Anti-HIV medications can reduce viral loads below infectious levels. In many of these cases, HIV was never transmitted, and the sex was consensual. Nonetheless, "offenders" can be recorded on provincial and national sex offender registries and held in segregation units, including administrative segregation—solitary confinement.

Imagine a world beyond these legal systems of domination. When on the defensive, activists often have no time to envision what else might address these diseases in proactive and more positive ways. Alternative ways of working are hard to see when your communities are dying, being locked up, or struggling to survive.

## THOUGHTS ON ANARCHISM AND RESPONSES TO HIV & HEPATITIS C

Many anarchist principles are active in our daily lives and our communities. In our responses to Hepatitis C and HIV, we fight for equitable access to medical knowledge and medications, bodily autonomy, and participation in decision-making. We seek interventions that are informed by lived experiences, emancipation from oppression, and the right to dignity for all people. Often those working in the Hepatitis C and HIV responses are unaware these goals are shared by anarchists. Those who do not understand anarchist theory often equate it with violence and destruction. However, anarchism seeks to build a non-coercive society, free of oppression and exploitation.

With our approach, we resist the modernist project of hyper-rational and universalizing forms of social organization rooted in a false paradigm of linear progress. Social organization and ideology not rooted in people's lived realities has the potential to be dangerous, oppressive, and violent. Ideology here refers to what queer radical Gary Kinsman coins as: "forms of knowledge that attends to managing people's lives that are not grounded in actual experiences & practices."[11] Anarchist scholar James C. Scott describes a "process-oriented" anarchist view, or anarchism through the integration of theory and practice.[12] Social problems are solved through a dialectical relationship between concerned groups of people over time. We can be flexible, fluid, responsive, spontaneous, and resistant to that which is solely ideological.

## THE VIOLENCE OF HIERARCHY & HOMOGENIZATION

Capitalist society organizes through homogenization and hierarchy—or forms of top-down social planning prescribing standardization. These processes are in settler-colonization, taxation, land ownership, urban planning, education, universal laws, and public health projects such as HIV and Hepatitis C "seek and treat" prevention as treatment initiatives. These are concerned with the "administration of things" through forms of centralized top-down social planning.[13] These systems are designed to displace local, traditional, and vernacular practices with hierarchical forms of organization. They mobilize technological mass surveillance aimed to quantify people's lives. This makes things more rational to higher authorities. Interventions then force a singular solution onto people, disconnected from local knowledge of daily lives. This social planning is counter to an anarchist worldview

interested in decentralization, heterogeneity, and respect for local knowledge and specificities.

Homogenization has been a major component of the grand modernist project of science. The natural world and the human body can be made knowable, classifiable, and rational through the work of highly trained "experts." Epidemic management can be possible through a system of surveillance, identification, containment, regulation, and control. The centralized management and standardization of information have helped us understand the scope of epidemics—who is most impacted and where. Although many people have been using cooperation and horizontal feminist organization since the beginning of the AIDS and Hepatitis C crises, over time, through financial coercion of granting systems, many conform to the standards of authorities. We have not seen many alternate forms of organizing responses to the two diseases.

Today, interventions must be "scaled-up," become official, systematized, credentialized, regulated, and organized hierarchically. For example, as governed by the United Nations, every country is supposed to have a top-down national AIDS strategy to prescribe programs of action for diverse local communities. These plans promote a singular ideological vision for how to respond to social problems without understanding their reality. Initiating hierarchical systems of representation (such as with the Country Coordinating Mechanisms of the Global Fund) limits the participation to representatives who "speak the language" and follow the rules. In this system, local cultures are seen as barriers, or in opposition to official "effective" and "rational" responses—and thus must be changed to make people's practices acceptable to universal norms.

One of the biggest current trends are massively funded country-wide "seek and treat" interventions. The B.C. Centre of "Excellence" on HIV/AIDS (quotations added) initiated this program in British Columbia, Canada to test populations of people deemed "at-risk" and provide treatment. Many of these people living in in Vancouver's Downtown Eastside are injection drug users living in poverty and without housing. In the program, if people test positive for HIV, they are immediately treated to prevent future transmissions. This approach is "treatment as prevention," a new norm of HIV intervention. In the "seek and treat" model, HIV testing fairs take place in public parks with a financial incentive to get tested. Overall, this intervention views people with HIV as vectors of disease who must be tested and treated to protect the general public. This approach is driven by paternalism, from a disconnected and extra-local plane of so-called reason and science.

People must make their own decision to initiate treatment. Anti-HIV drugs are a lifelong commitment, with possible side-effects. In the "seek and treat" intervention, the agency and autonomy of people living with HIV are undermined. People living with HIV are surveilled and coercively neutralized via anti-HIV treatments, incarceration, or quarantine (in prisons). For illicit drug users, the monitoring and surveillance of HIV treatment puts them at risk for arrest. For people who are homeless, taking medication every day may not be possible or a priority. The "seek and treat" intervention fails to address the lived realities of people who use drugs and live in poverty.

## CONCLUSION: ANARCHISM FOR HEALTH

"We live in a world that must be changed to survive"
—Zackie Achmat, South African AIDS activist[14]

There is not a singular solution to Hepatitis C and HIV. Mechanisms change how society will function and respond. Through ongoing dialogue, reflection and critical engagement without hierarchy, an anarchist approach ensures people's needs are met directly. We are inspired by the Nigerian women sex workers, participants in an early 2000s HIV treatment as prevention trial, which was deemed a failure by USAID and pharmaceutical company Gilead, maker of Truvada. Nigeria has a high-prevalence rate of HIV with limited treatment access. In the 1990s, as a condition to receive development grants, the United States demanded that Nigeria implement patent protection laws in the service of pharmaceutical company interests.[15] The result has widely restricted access to life-saving HIV medications. Truvada was being tested on HIV-negative women to prevent future HIV transmissions; in this context, it became rational for the HIV-negative women enrolled in the USAID and Gilead Truvada drug trial to keep all the medications for themselves (in case if they tested HIV-positive at a later date), or to distribute them to family members or friends living with HIV who needed them for immediate survival. The drug trial was discontinued, as accurate results on the use of the medications could not be determined. But the women supported themselves and their communities, despite the master plan. They enabled access to medication in an otherwise oppressive structure. While they may not have seen themselves as activists, these women supported the community in spite of the higher authority. These women realized anarchist principles and liberatory practices to support health.

In many places around the world, people who are unable to access government-funded Hepatitis C treatment use online chat forums and social media to advise one another how to legally access affordable forms of the medication from generic drug manufacturers or countries with cheaper drug prices. In the spirit of HIV buyers' clubs, virtual groups of so called "non-professionals" provide health support, subverting oppressive systems to get what they need. A course of treatment that can cost $94,000, can thus be accessed for around $1,000.[16] This approach to collectivity and mutual aid is central to mobilizing forms of anarchism for health.

When thinking through antihierarchical ways of doing things, endless planning and researching the response to HIV and Hepatitis C can easily get in the way. We question the drive to intervene in others' lives, and reflect on the power we hold in relation to others. Organizing should be local and come from the communities in question without hierarchy, without profiting off bodies and illnesses. A horizontal view trusts people will always innovate, cooperate, and look after each other.

The war on drugs, harm reduction, treatment access, criminalization, citizenship status, wealth inequity—all relate to hierarchical decision-making, liberal nation-states, and the capitalist organization of society. What could we get done if people accessed what they needed without a higher authority? How can we work to interrogate and reflect on how and why certain truths render certain social organizations possible, while others are rendered impossible, or too unrealistic? What if our society was not organized to view bodies as a source of capital? What if illness and disease were not a revenue stream for businesses, institutions, and a range of other actors? Imagine what our responses to health and HIV and Hepatitis C could look like if we did not battle against massive state, institutional, and private sector apparatuses for our survival.

## NOTES

1        B. Were, "The Destructive Strings of US Aid." *New York Times*. December 15, 2005.

2        This article and larger project was initiated with the support from the Institute for Anarchist Studies though the annual writers grant.

3        David P. Ball, "The Worst Enemy of a Government Is Its Own Population," Indymedia Beirut. Accessed May 13, 2006.

4        "How AIDS Has Changed Everything," Fact Sheet 2014 Global Statistics (Nd.)

5        For further readings and analysis on HIV, housing exclusion, and regulation, see: A. Guta, and M. Gagnon, "Spaces of Exclusion and Regulation: Housing Programs as Biopolitical Tools for the Management of People living with HIV," excerpt from presentation at the 10th International Conference on New Directions in the Humanities. June 14-16, 2012. Centre Mont-Royal, Montreal, Canada.

6        Caroline Chen, "Gilead Profit Tops Estimates as Hepatitis C Drug Sales Surge." *Bloomberg Business*. Accessed July 28, 2015.

7        Richard Knox, "$1,000 Pill for Hepatitis C Spurs Debate Over Drug Prices." National Public Radio. Accessed

February 6, 2014. NPR.

8      P. Barrett and R. Langreth. "Pharma Execs Don't Know Why Anyone is Upset by a $94,500 Miracle Cure." *Bloomberg Business Week*. Accessed June 3, 2015.

9      J. Grebely, "Low Uptake of Treatment for Hepatitis C Virus Infection in a Large Community-Based Study of Inner City Residents." *Journal of Viral Hepatitis*, No. 16 (2009): 352-358.

10     E. Mykhalovskiy, and G. Betteridge, "Who? What? Where? When? And with What Consequences? An Analysis of Criminal Cases of HIV Non-disclosure in Canada". *Canadian Journal of Law and Society*, No. 27 (1) (2012): 31–53.

11     G. Kinsman, "Vectors of Hope and Possibility: Commentary on Reckless Vectors." *Sexuality Research & Social Policy*, 2(2) (2005): 99-105.

12     J.C. Scott, *Two Cheers for Anarchism: Six Easy Pieces on Autonomy, Dignity, and Meaningful Work and Play*. Princeton, NJ: Princeton University Press, 2014.

13     Ibid.

14     Peter Piot, "AIDS: From Crisis Management to Sustained Strategic Response" *The Lancet*, Volume 368, August 5, 2006. Accessed February 24, 2016.

15     J. Peterson, "Ethical Misrecognition: The Early Prep Tenofovir Trial Failures." Presentation at Knowing Practices: the 2nd International Conference for the Social Sciences and Humanities in HIV. July 7-10, 2013 Paris, France.

16     Michael Atkin and Joel Keep. "Hep C Sufferer Imports Life Saving Drugs From India: Takes on Global Pharmaceutical Company." ABC News Australia. Accessed August 20, 2015.

## ABOUT THE AUTHORS

*Zoë and Alexander received an IAS writing grant to complete this work.*

*Zoë Dodd is a longtime harm reduction and Hepatitis C worker and activist. She has spent the last decade facilitating Hepatitis C support groups that are rooted in popular education and harm reduction. She was instrumental in developing a community-based model that prioritizes people who use drugs and are living with HIV/ Hepatitis C co-infection. Zoë is a feminist, anti-capitalist, and drug-user activist. She is an active member of the Toronto Harm Reduction Workers' Union, the Ontario Coalition Against Poverty, and AIDS ACTION NOW!*

*Alexander McClelland is a writer and doctorate student whose work focuses on the intersections of life, law and disease. He has developed a range of collaborative writing and activist projects that address issues of criminalization, sexual autonomy, surveillance, drug liberation, and the construction of knowledge on HIV and AIDS. Alexander is a member of AIDS ACTION NOW! and the PosterVirus affinity group.*

# BREAKING THE WAVES: CHALLENGING THE LIBERAL TENDENCY WITHIN ANARCHIST FEMINISM

## ROMINA AKEMI AND BREE BUSK

The Black Rose Anarchist Federation sent a delegation to participate in AFem2014, an international anarchist feminist conference developed by a committee of anarchists organizing in the UK. The goals of AFem2014 were to challenge sexism and other forms of oppression within the anarchist movement and to create a "safer space" to start conversations around individual and collective experiences that could be translated into organizing work. The conference committee hoped that the energy generated by this event would reinvigorate anarchist feminism as a whole, and would be reproduced as an ongoing series of conferences with a global impact. When viewed from this perspective, AFem2014 was an important political development that highlights the growth of anarchism and the need to advance the theory and practice of feminism within it. However, the Black Rose delegation left AFem2014 with more questions than answers, the foremost being, "What is anarchist feminism?"

As members of this delegation, we anticipated that the international nature of the conference would allow participants a unique opportunity to compare organizing strategies from different parts of the world and return home with new political relationships that would lay the groundwork for future coordination. Unfortunately, the conference was underdeveloped in several ways that limited this potential. The primary example was the conference committee's prioritization of developing rigorous attendance and safer space policies and simultaneous failure to apply this same rigor to the solicitation and development of the conference content. There was a great deal of weight placed on having the "right" people attend (those directly impacted by gendered oppression) and creating the "right" environment in which they could meet (one governed by a safer spaces policy designed to exclude oppressive behavior). These are not negative things in and of themselves, but we found that the hyperfocus placed on them to the exclusion of the intentional curation of the political content resulted in a representation of anarchist feminism that simultaneously included all politics and no politics.

AFem2014 lacked the ambition that would have allowed its potential to be realized. It was taken for granted that simply existing under patriarchy was a radical act and that this shared experience of oppression would be able to serve as a proxy for a shared political heritage and perspective. While we celebrate our own survival and that of our comrades, we are unwilling to settle for it. In fact, if we allow anarchist feminism to remain anchored in our identities rather than our practices, we risk being caught unprepared when challenges arise that demand more than a surface correction. For example, there were several occasions within the conference where the safer spaces policy would have been bolstered by a specific analysis regarding race and imperialism; the result was that a white participant wearing dreadlocks received a quick admonishment for cultural appropriation, but a complicated and painful incident regarding the silencing of a speaker relating experiences of gendered violence

in the Middle East went unaddressed.

In order to respond to the political crises of our day, anarchist feminism must be able to communicate with knowledge and conviction. Those of us who wish to develop this political tendency must locate ourselves within history and build upon the lessons of the past. We must develop new theories and test them in struggle. We must build mass movements and advocate for anarchism from within them. We must make demands, and, in the words of Italian anarchist Errico Malatesta, "take or win all possible reforms with the same spirit that one tears occupied territory from the enemy's grasp in order to go on advancing."[1] Finally, we must orient ourselves internationally and engage in solidarity with our global comrades. Through these practices, anarchist feminism can become a specific political force capable of confronting the formidable challenges set before us by capitalism and the state.

By definition, a broad feminist movement will not fully represent our politics. Instead, it will serve as an avenue to challenge and advance feminism where it is being made: on the streets, in our homes, at our jobs, in the media, and through our intricate and overlapping social networks. Pushing anarchist feminism out of our small collective spaces and into the social arena means that we are willing to struggle for relevance within the movements of the working class. Our politics are more than just useful tools for managing our personal lives; they represent the blueprints for a world worth fighting and dying for. Breaking the Waves is a call to break with liberal feminism and acknowledge the necessity of reconstructing our own anarchist feminist historical tradition. We are simultaneously declaring a need for anarchists who are feminists and feminists who are anarchists to discuss and debate what anarchist feminism means in practice and to refine that definition through renewed struggle. Our goal is not to provide a complete guide to a new anarchist feminism, but to advance a few steps beyond the vague politics that characterize this moment. We anticipate many readers will share the frustrations and ambitions of this article, based on our own experiences and conversations with comrades who have felt similarly constrained by an anarchist movement that lacks a meaningful feminist practice, and a feminist movement that declares collective struggle can only begin once we've purified ourselves and all those with whom we would organize. In the former, our politics are marginalized along with our voices. In the latter, there is no room for education to take place in struggle. The pressures of double militancy are exacerbated when our two political spaces compete for our time and labor. When we spoke to comrades within our own organizations, at AFem2014, and in all the other myriad contexts in which we encounter each other, there was a common theme expressed: we deserve better, and we are ready to fight for it. We hope that this article can be a factor in generating a productive, challenging conversation around the issues we've raised, and we are eager to engage with theoretical contributions and criticisms as they come.

## ANARCHIST FEMINISM

Anarchist feminism is a term that lacks a clear definition. In the US anarchist movement, it is employed so inconsistently that it is difficult to distill its meaning down to more than "antipatriarchal work done by anarchists, usually women." In a world where our revolutionary movements have rich histories of theory and struggle to draw from, we do not believe such a definition is sufficient. Since anarchist feminism lacks a narrative of unbroken collective struggle, it operates as an "edgier" form of feminism, which is most visible when confronting patriarchy in the realm of interpersonal interaction and can be measured by the experience of the individual and their ability to adapt to specific social behaviors and insular lifestyles. However, this lack of history and specificity has not prevented individuals or organizations from making significant political contributions in the name of anarchist feminism.

The publication of *Quiet Rumors: An Anarcha-Feminist Reader* (1978) marked an important step in elucidating the anarchist feminist tradition. By bringing together a diverse selection of authors and continuing to update the content through subsequent editions, the editors captured the fractured, often contradictory, and evolving politics that fall under the umbrella of anarchist feminism. A review by Red Sonja, a member of the Northeastern Federation of Anarchist Communists (NEFAC) notes, "If anarchism 'undefined' is the sprawling body of thought that it is, reaching such polar philosophical distances as rugged individualism on one hand and libertarian communism on the other, then 'anarcha-feminism' also covers such a vast political terrain with fuzzy boundaries."[2] Unfortunately, many of the essays contained in *Quiet Rumors* stand in isolation, lacking a coherent thread to follow from one idea to the next. In the preface to the third edition, author Roxanne Dunbar-Ortiz celebrates the recentering of female anarchist heroines and states, "Our task as anarcha-feminists can be nothing less than changing the world and to do that we need to consult our heroic predecessors."[3] And yet, it is often the case that anarchist feminism is defined exclusively by these female revolutionaries at the expense of understanding them in the context of the organizations and movements in which they operated.

As an anarchist who spoke and wrote at length about the oppression of women, Emma Goldman is the first (and often the last) name that comes to mind when thinking of anarchist feminism. She was anything but an individualist and overemphasizing her as such misplaces her historically. In the US, she was politically active in the Industrial Workers of the World (IWW), she participated in the struggle to legalize birth control, as well as the antiwar movement during the First World War. Goldman continues to be influential within anarchism because of her notable impact within larger movements and historical events, and it is a mistake to view her exclusively as a romantic figure that is commonly misquoted as declaring, "If I can't dance, I don't want to be part of your revolution." There are several contemporary anarchists that stand beside Goldman in her place of prominence, such as Lucy Parsons and Voltairine De Cleyre. It is rare for organizations to rise to the level of feminist celebrity achieved by the aforementioned individuals, but even anarchists uninterested in the historical struggle of women can be counted on to know Mujeres Libres, a women's organization that fought for gender equality during the Spanish Civil War

(1936-1939). The tendency to view our politics as exemplified by valorized individuals leaves us open to many pitfalls. First, we are encouraged to imagine the politics of these individuals as frozen in time, rather than as a product of a lifetime of experiential learning. Second, by binding ourselves to individuals rather than specific political theories and practices, we are forced to find a way to ignore their inevitable failings or be willing to discard them completely as imperfect avatars of prefiguration. The truth is that in many cases, the gender of our predecessors is the least interesting thing about them. We will serve them better (and in doing so, serve ourselves better) by placing them in their proper historical context and studying how they navigated the political challenges of their day.

Anarchist feminism has failed to develop a politics that is distinct from liberal feminism, socialist/Marxist feminisms, or radical feminism. Instead, it signals the rejection of the sexist culture found in previous generations of political work without ever clarifying a positive vision of how we are to shape our movements, or which theories and tactics are best suited to our goals. Without a revolutionary ideology to illuminate the path towards ever-increasing challenges to the state and capitalism, individuals in these spaces are left with few choices but to turn forever inward, raising their consciousness, but to no higher purpose. And yet, there is a collective desire within anarchism to struggle against patriarchy. At every turn, we are told that the solution is an individual one. But here, we anarchists and aspiring anarchist feminists agree with Carol Hanisch in her seminal article, "The Personal is Political":

"There are no personal solutions at this time. There is only collective action for a collective solution."[4]

## THE LIMITS OF WAVE THEORY AND ACADEMIC FEMINISM: WHAT IS OUR HISTORICAL AND POLITICAL LINEAGE?

Academic feminists have cataloged the history of feminist movements in the US into three progressive waves. The First Wave centered on the struggle for suffrage in the early twentieth century. The Second Wave—known as the Women's Liberation Movement—developed in the 1960s and '70s around the fight to legalize abortion and the failed demand for an Equal Rights Amendment (ERA). Finally, the Third Wave continues to function as a critique of the white and heteronormative politics of Second Wave discourse and represents a shift from a movement-based politics to a more individual approach. Since it lacks grounding in a particular struggle, the ideas and practices of this wave persist without a clear conclusion. This Western conception of modern feminist history is broadly understood and accepted, and yet, there is still a great deal of debate around the precise character of each wave and how they impact the feminisms of today. Even now, there is a scramble to define a Fourth Wave in relation to women's participation in emerging technologies. However, as anarchists and feminists working within a revolutionary tradition, we cannot trace our lineage through individualist, liberal, or academic formations of feminism.

Many anticapitalist, revolutionary women have been conveniently left out of academic texts and histories. In the late nineteenth and early twentieth centuries, socialist women had little association with First Wave feminism because of its bourgeois component and reformist framework. In the UK, where the suffrage movement had a larger working-class base and utilized more militant tactics, there was more political interaction.[5] University feminist theory courses rarely entertain critiques of the suffrage movement, which *ipso facto* erases the activities of these revolutionary women. Instead, they celebrate the accomplishments of the First Wave and place it within the narrative of historical progress. But was it progress when white suffrage organizers refused to include Black suffrage fighters such as Ida B. Wells? The history of feminism is full of these contradictions that stand as important learning experiences. As we search for the words and actions from which to construct our tradition, we will find affinity in both familiar and unlikely places, including the traditions of Marxist and liberal feminisms. Building an anarchist feminist historical tradition will give us a platform to advance our own politics, understand our work in the context of what has already been done, and then forge ahead. Anarchist feminists who seek to reconstruct their political tradition must navigate carefully, and even bravely sail into foreign waters. We have always existed, but we have not always been seen.

In *Black Flame: The Revolutionary Class Politics of Anarchism and Syndicalism*, the authors state, "We admit a certain discomfort with the tendency of many writers to label women anarchists and syndicalists, 'anarchist feminists,' or 'anarcha-feminists.'"[6] We share their discomfort. This practice reflects a trend that emerged among Second Wave historians and activists who began to search for women in history. Some began to retroactively label strong and independent women from the historical past as feminists, reinforcing an ahistorical understanding of feminism. Furthermore, these writers and theorists failed in offering a dialectical analysis of feminism, the meaning of which has changed over the last one hundred plus years. During the Second Wave feminist movement in the US, a political shift occurred as many socialist women infused the feminist ideology of the era with their anticapitalist and revolutionary views. While there were a handful of socialist and anarchist women who used the feminist label in the late nineteenth and early twentieth centuries, the vast majority did not. This was because feminism emerged as a movement that represented the needs of bourgeois and upper middle class women who wanted the same access to citizen rights and professional opportunities as their male counterparts.

Debating the retroactive use and misuse of feminism is not a petty dispute over terms and hyphenation, but a matter of political import. First, not doing so places all feminisms as part of the same family and reinforces gender over class and political affiliation. Second, it erases entire political legacies, especially revolutionary traditions that functioned outside of, and sometimes against, the waves. The majority of socialist and anarchist women cannot escape the feminist hyphenation that reminds everyone of their gender. Additionally, this practice of finding "feminists" in history creates a false consciousness that reinforces the notion that some women are "unaware" of their feminism, while women who fall outside of expected feminist behaviors are labeled

"unsisterly" or "patriarchal women."[7] There are some women who support patriarchy, but the vast majority has to negotiate and compromise to survive within this patriarchal and capitalist society. Finally, by not placing various feminisms within their historical context, the ideological core of feminism is softened and dispersed to the point that it ceases to be a collection of theories and practices and is instead replaced by a timeless, transcendent feeling that even the likes of Hillary Clinton can draw on. There is a growing need to reaffirm feminism as a political ideology in order to rebuild a movement in which ideas can be debated and radical theory can flourish as praxis.

## LA ALZADA: ACCIÓN FEMINISTA LIBERTARIA (CHILE)

The word *alzada* is the feminine form of the Spanish noun that means rebel, instigator, or escalator. The term "territorial work" refers to community and housing work, emphasizing a geographic location. The term "libertarian" is used interchangeably with "anarchist" in Latin America and Spain. The use of the word "militant" refers to a member of a revolutionary organization that meets an expected level of political activity. Anarchist *especifista* organizations, such as the Uruguayan Anarchist Federation (FAU), promote the creation of specific (especifista) anarchist organizations for political work and use the strategy of social insertion for participation in social movements. "Social insertion" means building a base for anarchist ideas inside unions and other social organizations while emphasizing horizontal political participation. The term "multisectoralism" is a term used by the Chilean Left—see endnote 20 for definition.

On March 9, 2013, a group of anarchist feminists in Santiago, Chile announced the formation of La Alzada. La Alzada is not the only libertarian feminist organization in Chile, neither before nor after its foundation. However, we chose to highlight La Alzada because their organizational goal of building libertarian feminism is aligned with our own political vision. It is important to note that the backdrop of La Alzada's foundation was the growth and emergence of an anarchist movement over two decades. Concurrently, the impact of feminist and queer politics were also being felt within the revolutionary Left. Organizations such as *Coordinadora Universitaria por la Disidencia Sexual* (CUDS, Sexual Dissidence University Coordinator) and *La Champurria* (meaning "mixture" in Mapudungun) reflect the arrival of a queer social movement and new dialogues about feminism and queerness.[8] The practices of La Alzada reflect three significant elements we wish to highlight: the importance of doing social movement and social insertion work; making their politics present and influential within the Left; and the creation of new theory.

In order to contextualize La Alzada's work, it is necessary to explain the political meaning and significance of sexual dissidence. The term sexual dissidence has a particular meaning and genealogy within Chilean feminism, queer, and social movements. Sexual dissidence is a critique of patriarchy and heteronormativity, as well as the LGBTQ (Lesbian, Gay, Bisexual, Transgender, Queer) movement in its

alliance with the state. Some in this movement have ceased to question the socialization of violence and instead seek reforms such as marriage equality and antidiscrimination laws.[9] The term also functions as a counterpoint to the concept of sexual diversity that emphasizes the struggle for civil rights and inclusion within the capitalist state, instead of challenging the existence of patriarchy. The most well-known sexual dissidence collective is CUDS, which defines their work in this way: "There are no women, men, or gays here. We are [the ones who] the feminist wave in Santiago, Chile threw away. Officially we are a postfeminist sexual dissident university collective that organizes our bodies to perform sexual terror actions within spaces of sexual authoritarianism."[10] CUDS organizes political interventions to spark conversation, instigate controversy, and question the social parameters that patriarchy has normalized. In November, 2012, CUDS organized a protest at the National Encounter of Diverse Feminists after a CUDS member was prevented from participating for being a "bio-male."[11] CUDS went to the congress and placed a banner outside that stated "*Feminismo en Toma*" ("Feminism Occupied") to bring attention to a growing feminist movement that sought to challenge both masculinity and transphobia, in which CUDS called for a "feminism without women."[12] At the July 25, 2013 feminist march demanding the legalization of abortion, CUDS marched with a banner that stated, "*El Derecho a No Nacer*" ("The Right to Not Be Born"), playing a prominent role during the occupation of the national cathedral in downtown Santiago. Other banners included: "Sodomize Heteropatriarchy with Your Clitoris" and "Abort Like Animals." The sexual dissidence movement has also lead to the growth of transfeminism in Chile, taking on a similar role in politicizing trans commitment to building and intervening within the feminist movement and against patriarchy.

La Alzada's defining divergence from other feminist groups is that they are a social political organization in which membership requires a predetermined level of political activity.[13] An Alzada militant participates in insertion work with working-class women and within the student movement, and advances their own political interventions within the anarchist and feminist movements. Membership is open to all and they encourage the inclusion of male-identified militants. They work closely with the domestic worker unions SINTRACAP and SINAICAP that are divided by Chilean-born (the former) and foreign-born (the latter) members who mostly hail from Peru and Bolivia. They organize union workshops, such as teaching oral and bodily expressions to build confidence and political development for rank-and-file members.[14] They have used Theatre of the Oppressed—an interactive technique used to promote social change and critique—as a tool to analyze experiences with oppression and develop combative ideas.[15] They also participated in the January, 2014 port workers' strike that had a mostly male base. They received criticism from some feminists for their participation, but La Alzada's response was that it was important to be present in a major labor struggle. It allowed them to engage with workers and discuss their feminist work while offering solidarity.[16] They view this type of work as part of building

feminist unionism that simultaneously challenges the feminist, labor, and anarchist movements.

The student movement is another key site of political activity. Prior to the split within the *FEL* (*Frente de Estudiantes Libertario*—Libertarian Student Front), an anarchist student federation, many Alzada members were also FEL militants. In 2013 the FEL decided to run a coalition ticket with other Left student federations for the presidency of the university student federation, *CONFECH* (*Confederación de Estudiantes de Chile*). Melissa Sepulveda, who is a member of La Alzada and was a member of FEL (she now participates in Acción Libertaria), won the presidency under a libertarian and feminist campaign. The propaganda material included the slogan, "Democratize the University...De-Masculinize Politics!" Sepulveda used her position as head of CONFECH to deepen a multisectoral approach.[17] Multisectoral politics create bonds of solidarity and work within the various sectors of political activity (labor, territorial, and education). Sepulveda also promoted the demand for a *Universidad No Sexista* (Non-Sexist University). This call was originally made at the 1981 meeting by the Network for Popular Education Among Women (REPM).[18] With the support of various feminist and Leftist organizations, the First Congress for a Non-Sexist Education took place in September, 2014. Congress organizers sought to begin a dialogue and develop concrete proposals to confront the institutionalization of gender and sexual discrimination and patriarchal politics within the education system.[19] The congress document, synthesizing their discussion outlines, identified the themes and demands. One of these was for the building of an educational project that questioned the sexist and heteronormative logic inherent in the education system. Their final demand exemplifies their broader political framework: "To strengthen the networks within feminism and coordinate with other social actors (workers, *pobladores*[20], indigenous peoples, etc.) and to pose in all spheres a project of free education that is high quality, nonsexist, nonreligious, intercultural, and in the service to the people."[21]

Finally, La Alzada's work is characterized by their commitment to politically intervene within the anarchist and revolutionary Left movements in Chile. In a 2013 interview, La Alzada explains:

> Many anarchist and Leftist organizations with revolutionary intent attempt to revalorize women, especially working-class women as doubly exploited. Most of the time it doesn't go farther than a pamphlet, which doesn't create a concrete praxis. From the subordination of women to control over our body to a critique of the family—such issues are part of the propaganda of various newsletters, articles, and bulletins within the broader fights of anarchism. However, these will matter little if we do not deepen our [political] positions. The idea of "the emancipation of women" becomes stale without the inclusion of a feminist framework within those same organizations. The creation of La Alzada outlines the necessity for two jobs: on the one hand, we have a responsibility within libertarian spaces and, on the other hand, the need to reach out and do territorial work from a gender perspective within those social and public spaces.[22]

This framework simultaneously challenges feminist separatism and those who criticize revolutionary feminists for investing their time and energy in building political organizations. La Alzada frames their interventions and development of feminist and anarchist praxis within other movements as necessary to their revolutionary commitment. If we consider anarchist spaces or the labor movement as "not worth it," then why bother calling ourselves anarchist feminists?

## THE BACKDROP TO CONTEMPORARY FEMINIST POLITICS

The 1990s marked a political shift in global politics, as well as in anarchist and feminist organizing. The fall of the Soviet Union led to a mass disillusionment with Leninist politics, but it was also a moment of political reorganization for global capitalism. The lack of an adversary allowed for the expansion of neoliberal policies proposed by the Washington Consensus.[23] The Washington Consensus was a term coined in 1989 in a piece written by John Williamson. It described the political and economic policies that were being debated in Washington to usher in a new post-Cold War era and the eventual expansion of economic policies that later became known as neoliberalism. The economic arena met the social when attacks on social reforms became necessary for streamlining these policies. In the US, there was a consolidation of the neoliberal economic order with

Evangelical Christian ideology that, in turn, generated the so-called Culture Wars. Among others, Rush Limbaugh, who became a central figure in the 1990s, used Italian Marxist Antonio Gramsci's theory of cultural war to reverse the social gains of the previous thirty years. Feminists were unprepared for such a challenge.[24]

Right wing social movements such as Operation Rescue emerged from this period and made the criminalization of abortion their central rallying call.[25] Liberal feminist organizations such as the National Organization for Women (NOW) offered minimal response and, instead, pushed to expunge the use of the word "abortion" from its propaganda. Higher costs and a service consolidation into urban areas meant the private clinic model limited the availability of reproductive services.

In the 1990s, women had little choice but to defend narrow gains.[26] This marked the end of an offensive women's movement that sought to expand rights and a transition to a defensive one that desperately struggled to retain the gains of the previous decade. It is helpful to note that the feminist punk scene of Riot Grrrl emerged at the same time that Operation Rescue was shutting down abortion clinics and Bill Clinton was reversing "welfare as we know it." Riot Grrrl was a political response to the frustrations of a new generation facing a moment of political weakness and disappointment. A cultural movement such as Riot Grrrl offered a much-needed critique of male-dominated spaces, yet was confined to a limited audience. This era also introduced organizations such as INCITE! (founded in 2000) whose work focused on community

accountability and restorative justice as a response to the massive expansion of the prison industrial complex (PIC) during the 1990s. Many of the founders of INCITE! came out of Critical Resistance, a California-based prison abolition organization. However, the decline of social movements capable of resisting neoliberalism generated a tendency towards self-reflection, and the creation of projects with a limited scope and base of participants.[27]

Since the 1990s, there has been an expansion of feminist and queer theory in universities. Works such as *Gender Trouble: Feminism and the Subversion of Identity* (1990) by Judith Butler and *Feminism is for Everybody: Passionate Politics* (2000) by bell hooks had a strong influence on feminist politics and offered recognition of queer politics. Academia became a place where feminism could flourish, but it also became increasingly disconnected from the struggles of working-class people due to its isolation within classrooms. In the last few years, movements such as Occupy Wall Street and Black Lives Matter have emerged. While elements of college-based feminism are visible within the practices of these movements, the effect was minimal. This type of feminism was not designed to thrive outside the walls of the academy. College-based feminism can be credited with introducing some feminist ideas to the mainstream. For example, the issue of rape on college campuses has recently been acknowledged by the Obama administration and is being discussed in many major media outlets, providing opportunities for radical narratives, such as education around rape culture and pushback against slut shaming and catcalling. New feminists are analyzing the systemic impact of patriarchy on their own lives, but their framing too often reflects the experiences and demands of a particular political actor: the college student. The result of this limitation is a culture that prioritizes symbolic action and online debate over collective struggle.[28] The emphasis on the individual experience of patriarchy, and individual responses, reflects the depth with which liberal politics has affected US feminist activism. But this focus on the individual does not take into consideration the broader hardships that women, queer, genderqueer, and transgender folks experience on the job and within working-class communities.

Our search for a pure prefiguration has grown into a collective practice of hyper-vigilance in which callout culture has emerged as a new power structure. It is most visible in online feminist and queer communities localized in social media sites such as Tumblr. The so-called "social justice warriors" often use public shaming and individual promotion to develop political clout. This has reinforced a purist activist approach in which there is no differentiation between someone who is trying to understand political terminology and chauvinistic, transphobic trolls. Where we differ is not on the importance of prefiguration, but with the interpretation of prefiguration as a state of fixed purity instead of an ideal we are always in the process of realizing. In the meantime, the feminist movement offers little threat to the status quo and continues to idle in the stagnant waters of liberal politics.

## BEFORE WE TAKE IT ALL, WE DEMAND THE FOLLOWING

As anarchist communists committed to intersectional class struggle (meaning our organizing reflects an analysis of how different forms of oppression and exploitation interact), our feminist praxis is informed by a political lineage that provides us with tools for understanding and advancing our struggles against capitalist patriarchy. We can draw on the lessons of the Paris Commune, Russian Revolution, and Spanish Civil War. Simultaneously, we can engage with the emerging theories and practices of the global South. US anarchists in particular need not restrict our revolutionary education to the classroom when there are opportunities to learn from comrades actively testing exciting, new methods of engagement in the Americas. By using the especifista tactic of social insertion, we can introduce our politics in an authentic way that has the ability to expand and escalate as struggles intersect. While making social demands on the state is frequently denounced as a reformist tactic, certain reforms can improve and save the lives of working people and strategically develop our revolutionary capacity. The struggle to achieve these types of immediate victories can generate a practice of cross-movement solidarity, and, eventually, challenge the political arena of the state in which we can influence the rhythm of politics, rather than simply chase or react to bourgeois politics. In order to act effectively in these broad coalitions, we must have a clear understanding of, and commitment to, our own politics. We must be prepared to consider which demands can bear compromise and which must retain their explicit, radical character.

In synthesizing the sections about La Alzada and the recent historical background, there are several points we want to underscore. The outlining of the US feminist movement since the 1990s is meant to place where we stand today historically. The general attitude towards feminism in the US is that we are preparing eulogies for whom the bell tolls. Articles such "The War on Women Is Over—and Women Lost" in Mother Jones recap the loss of reproductive rights over the last few decades.[29] These articles often leave out the current social movements in the US that can be the basis for articulating a new feminist politics brewing in the margins.[30] La Alzada offers an example of an anarchist feminist organization that is committed to both internal and external work, including new gender theories (such as sexual dissidence) within a class struggle framework. In many anarchist and Leftist organizations, attempts are made to demonstrate solidarity with the fight against patriarchy by showing strong support for feminist concerns and proposals. Yet, the tactic of "voting for feminism" often comes to nothing due to minimal support, and/or the lack of proposals to implement ongoing internal work, including the failure to build the political capacity of female, transgender, and queer comrades. We need more than feminism on paper; we need an antipatriarchal commitment in our internal and external activities. La Alzada's areas of work reflect demands for the legalization of abortion, sexual reproductive and non-reproductive rights, and for non-sexist education. They also challenge assumptions around strategic sector organizing, offering an intervention to rupture the patriarchal capitalist system.[31] [32]

Breaking the Waves calls for a break with liberal feminism, citing the tendency for liberal feminism's political dominance to stall the development of revolutionary feminist theory and praxis. We want to move beyond defensive demands and self-criticism that reflect a scramble for the crumbs that the system has offered. Instead, we want to redirect the flow of our political energy into building movements that go on the offensive to simultaneously improve our daily lives through social demands, while prefiguring the type of society we wish to construct. This also means treating our smaller campaigns as opportunities to learn and train for the long war against patriarchal capitalism. We have the political energy and desire to fight, but we have not learned how to maximize that flow of energy in a revolutionary way.

A movement needs achievable goals and a reason for an individual to invest time, energy and, possibly, their life. Some of us are driven by strong ideological commitments, while others participate based on issues that directly affect our personal and familial life. The process of identifying these commonalities will be the bloodline to a broader movement that is both intersectional and intersectoral.[33] The rebuilding of a feminist movement that is committed to fighting colonialism and patriarchal capitalism has to engage with broader social issues. We want to move beyond the cycle of what we are against because there is so much that we would like to create. We view this list of demands as a work in progress: seeds that need the nutrients of a collective movement to give them life and meaning. The following is a list of our initial demands:

★ Universal healthcare;

★ Support for reproductive and non-reproductive rights through the creation of reproductive, sexual, and gender-based service clinics, including free abortion on demand, in all public hospitals, and in geographically isolated locations;

★ Support for reproductive services for individuals who wish to have or adopt children. This includes free community childcare facilities, available food programs in the neighborhood and at school. These programs also encourage breaking down masculine gender roles and expectations in relation to family and community care;

★ Services for survivors of gendered violence, including housing, therapy, and access to mental health services;

★ Rehabilitation services for sex offenders, including group and individual therapy;

★ That all healthcare and related services be provided with respect, knowledge, and compassion to those who seek them, regardless of gender, sexual practices, relationship type, or family model;

★ Parental leave, family emergency leave, rights and resources for domestic care, fully accessible services in the home and in public for people with disabilities;

★ Expansion of government-funded housing; access to quality housing that enhances the ability of community interactions through design and provisional resources that meets the many needs and safety of those who will live there;

★ Community control of spaces and resources to better achieve the goals of that community. It is important for this organizing to stem from community organiz and assemblies, differentiate' from community spaces th do charity work that limits . autonomous and self-organizing capacity of working-class communities;

★ Full autonomy for indigenous peoples and the provision of resources free of cost; After hundreds of years of colonial oppression and resource exploitation, indigenous communities must be given full control over their land and livelihood. Resources needed to rebuild their communities as they see fit must be given as minimal compensation. This includes cleaning up mining waste and the return of stolen land. There are many other demands presented by indigenous communities in resistance and they should all be met;

★ The socialization of education; The expansion of education for all (no matter their age) as a social right, instead of a privilege;

★ Sex, antisexist, and interpersonal education; addressing the need for an interdisciplinary method of education that teaches children and teenagers about sex education and challenges patriarchal gender norms; The Non-Sexist Education campaigns in Latin America and Spain offer examples of how to promote and push for an antipatriarchal, anticapitalist, and anticolonial education system;

★ Revocation of the Taft-Hartley Act and Smith-Connally Act. Both of these acts were passed in the 1940s to hamper the gains and political weight of the labor movement following the organizing campaigns of the CIO in the 1930s and the strike waves following World War II (when 25 percent of the labor force was unionized). While we think we should organize no matter the legality given to us by the state, revoking these acts will give the working class breathing room to self-organize and strike. These acts currently prohibit wildcat strikes, secondary boycotts, solidarity strikes, and federal employees from striking. They further allow the federal government during wartime to seize and control an industry in which the workers have threatened, or are on, strike;

★ The decriminalization of sex work and support for the horizontal self-organization of sex workers;

★ That undocumented workers be fully protected by American labor laws, and that the enactment of these rights not be punishable by deportation; also, that the laws are expanded and additional resources are made available to address ;gender-based workplace inequalities and harassment

★ The abolition of state sanctioned marriage, which seeks to define relationships and families through the allocation of benefits and social acceptance;

★ Freedom for all people from intimidation by the threat or use of gendered violence; an end to the laws, assumptions and institutions that perpetuate patriarchal dominance and aggression; an immediate intervention to defend the lives of those existing at the intersections of multiple oppressions, who are disproportionately at risk of harm or death;

## CONCLUSION

We have outlined the need for a return to building feminist mass movements and the instigation of fresh anarchist ideas and tactics within emerging struggles. But as we formulate our role and our demands, we also need to consider how and where anarchist feminism has something to offer these movements. Through a re-investigation of our revolutionary heritage, and a principled engagement with the exciting new theories and practices of our global comrades, we can continue to transition from our small collectives and online communities to a position of consolidated political strength. This process will allow us to combat experiences of individual hardship with collective struggle and eventually contest the hegemonic power of capitalism and the state. If anarchist feminism fails to adapt to the challenges of our political moment, we must resign ourselves to a decade of think pieces documenting the rollback of the few remaining rights hard won by the social movements of our predecessors. We deserve better and we are ready to fight for it.

## NOTES

1    Errico Malatesta, "Reformism," *Life and Ideas: The Anarchist Writings of Errico Malatesta* (Oakland: PM Press, 2015)

2    "Book Review: Quiet Rumors: An Anarcha-Feminist Reader," Common Struggle/Lucha Común, April 20, 2003

3    Dark Star Collective, *Quiet Rumors: An Anarcha-Feminist Reader* (Oakland: AK Press, 2008), p. 11.

4    Carol Hanisch, "The Personal is Political," *Notes from the Second Year: Women's Liberation* (New York: Radical Feminism, 1970)

5    Nym Mayhall, Laura E. *The Militant Suffrage Movement: Citizenship and Resistance in Britain, 1860-1930.* (Oxford: Oxford University Press, 2003).

6    Michael Schmidt and Lucien van der Walt, *Black Flame: The Revolutionary Class Politics of Anarchism and Syndicalism* (Oakland: AK Press, 2009), 23.

7    Susan Faludi, "The Death of a Revolutionary: Shulamith Firestone helped to create a new society. But she couldn't live in it," *The New Yorker*, April 15, 2013

8    For information on CUDS: http://disidenciasexual.tumblr.com/

9    The italicized area is a direct quote by one of the authors of this article who translated an interview with La Alzada. See: Gutiérrez D., José Antonio. "La Alzada: 'The revolution must include the feminist struggle, with and inside the libertarian,'" Ideas and Action, October 25, 2013

10    http://disidenciasexual.tumblr.com/

11    http://revistacortela.com/la-rebelion-de-la-masculinidad/

12    http://www.pueg.unam.mx/images/seminarios2015_2/otras_rutas/sesion2/por_un_feminismo_sin_mujeres_cuds.pdf

13    For a definition on the social political organization, see Gutiérrez D., José Antonio. "The Problems Posed by the Concrete Class Struggle & Popular Organization: Reflections from the Anarchist Communist Perspective." Anarkismo.net. November 14, 2005.

14    La Alzada-AFL, "Construyendo feminismo sindical: taller de oratoria y expresión corporal con el Sintracap." *Solidaridad: Periódico Comunista Libertario Solidaridad*, 16 de noviembre del 2013.

15    The Brazilian theatre director Augusto Boal developed Theatre of the Oppressed in the 1950s.

16    La Alzada-AFL, Solidaridad Feminista con el Conflicto Portuario Hacia una Sindicalismo de clase, de lucha y feminista, enero 2014

17    Multisectoralism is a term used in the Chilean Left. The three main sectors are labor, territorial, and student movement. Multisectoralism means having a cross-sectoral analysis in offering solidarity support for demands and actions in other sectors. The Mapuche struggle is also considered another sector but autonomous. The environment, feminism, and colonialism are not considered separate sectors but transversal issues that must be included into the other sectors.

18    http://www.cladem.org/campanas/educacion-no-sexista/prensa/69-ens-otros-medios/443-dia-internacional-de-la-educacion-no-sexista

19    http://eldesconcierto.cl/por-que-es-necesaria-una-educacion-sexista-en-chile/

20    The word "población" is best defined as shantytown or poor working-class neighborhood. But poblaciones around Santiago have their own political history since they evolved as land takeovers by people who migrated from the countryside to the city. Some poblaciones have strong political and Leftist traditions, such as La Legua, Villa

Francia, and Nueva Amanecer. An individual who lives in a población is referred to as a poblador/a.

21    This demand not only synthesizes positions put forward by the feminist, indigenous, and queer movements, but also reflect the radical demand for the socialization of education being put forward by sections of the student movement.

22    José Antonio Gutiérrez D., "La Alzada: "The revolution must include the feminist struggle, with and inside the libertarian," *Ideas and Action*, October 6, 2013

23    See John Williamson, "A Short History of the Washington Consensus"

24    Charlie Bertsch, "Gramsci Rush: Limbaugh on the Culture War," *Bad Subjects*, 1994

25    Isabel Wilkerson, "Drive Against Abortion Finds a Symbol: Wichita," *New York Times*. August 4, 1991

26    Molly Redden, "The War on Women is Over—And Women Lost," *Mother Jones*, September/October 2015

27    During the mid to late 1990s, California experienced several social movements, including immigrant rights rallies, opposition to the expansion of the prison system, and large rallies in support of Mumia Abu Jamal. However, these movements became smaller following the 1999 World Trade Organization (WTO) protest in Seattle and by 2002 the focus became the antiwar movement.

28    One of the main debates happening on college campuses is about the use of trigger warnings. See: Rani Neutill. "My trigger-warning disaster: "9 1/2 Weeks," "The Wire" and how coddled young radicals got discomfort all wrong," *Salon*, Oct. 28, 2015; Nikki Calderon and Derek Wakefield.

29    Redden, "The War on Women Is Over—and Women Lost," *Mother Jones*.

30    Chris Dixon, *Another Politics: Talking Across Today's Transformative Movements*

(Berkeley: University of California Press Books, 2014).

31    Strategic sectors are sectors given priority. See note 20.

32    Patriarchal capitalism is a specific term used by La Alzada militants to force a strategic building dialogue that analyzes capitalism and patriarchy as interwoven systems and not in stages.

33    We are placing two political terms used in different places. Intersectional is used in the US and the UK. Intersectoral (or multisectoral) is used in Chile. Intersectional calls for an analysis that includes identity, race, and class. Multisectoralism includes those aspects but places the emphasis of sectors (labor, territorial, student movement) as the basis for political action, reinforcing social movement building.

## ABOUT THE AUTHORS

*Romina Akemi is a member of Black Rose Anarchist Federation (USA) and Solidaridad - Federación Comunista Libertaria (Chile). She was a garment industrial seamstress for many years, engaging in union and political organizing. She has also participated in many international socialist and anarchist gatherings over the years that have informed her internationalist perspective.*

*Bree Busk is an American anarchist living and working in Santiago, Chile. As a member of both Black Rose Anarchist Federation (USA) and Solidaridad - Federación Comunista Libertaria (Chile), she is dedicated to building international coordination across the Americas. She currently contributes to movements in both countries through art, organizing, and providing the invisible, reproductive labor that organizations need to survive and flourish.*

I am a human being in an era of robots, so don't judge my worth or my right to a full life solely on productivity at work.

I am not a machine; I need to spend my time doing what I love, & creating revolutions of the mind & heart.

# RADICAL LANGUAGE IN THE MAINSTREAM

## KELSEY CHAM C.

**A**s a person who did not come to radical perspectives from academia, I've had quite the challenge trying to find community with people whose politics I respect.

I grew up in the suburb of Newton, Surrey, territory of the Katzie, Kwantlen, Semiahmoo and Tsawwassen peoples. I was an athlete and last-minute procrastinator who never understood why school should be taken seriously. Though I read newspapers every day, I didn't have the words to describe the injustices I could see and feel. My lack of trust in the school system, and my dwindling trust in the politics of high level sports led me to believe I didn't need validation from institutions. In grade 8, I started skipping class to find freedom. A couple of years later I found myself getting into hard drugs and failing classes. Eventually, I failed out of high school completely and was pretty proud about it.

More than a missing diploma, more than my struggle with addiction, my biggest barrier to finding community in radical circles was a lack of exposure to their social expectations. I found very little compassion and support, and was often met with harsh judgment. Coming into these communities, I felt not smart enough and like an outcast. It took me years to understand the everyday language used in radical activist

Art by Bec Young | justseeds.org

communities. Some words were long, some were short, but everyone said these words so casually I thought I would come across as stupid to ask what they meant. I'd go to talks and workshops, and some really smart dude would talk for an hour and then open up the space for questions. I remember feeling so lost by the jargon that by the end, I didn't even know what the talk had been about. Clearly, I wasn't going to ask the questions running around in my brain. "What do you mean by colonization?" "What is queer theory?" "Who is Marx!?" "Why are you speaking to us like my boring geography teacher?"

Although I experienced some pretty traumatizing and violent times in my high school years and early twenties, I also experienced a lot of care, openness, respect, and trust. I will never forget the time I was hanging out at this meth house in a room covered in paranoid sharpie scribble - thoughts about death, killing, being followed, and the devil. The woman whose room we were in was smoking gak from a glass pipe, telling me about her brain tumors. Her teenage daughter came in to share a hit. After I left their house, they called me to let me know I left my zip lock bag with a few hundred dollars of meth in their bathroom. They didn't judge me for being senseless or even take advantage by keeping my stash. When I came back to retrieve it, they let me know how much they appreciated the energy I brought to their home and invited me to come over whenever I liked. They had generosity, openness, and care in their spirit.

My addicted self has gotten me into a lot of intense, violent, and traumatizing situations. However, during my addiction, I also experienced caring dynamics in relationships with other addicts. In contrast, those kinds of relationships have taken a really long time to find in self-identified radical communities. Respect for one another was of highest value, and we watched each other's backs. As much as there was fighting, people also had a lot of capacity for forgiveness. People would cheat, fight, rip each other off and then in a few months they would be chilling and having a good time. We'd help each other out even with little things. If I took too long in the bathroom my friend would text me, "There's nothing in your eye!" and I'd remember I was hallucinating so I would stop picking it.

When I came out as queer in Montreal, and as I got more and more clean, I started to find accurate words to describe how I felt about the world. Even though this skill was my entry into more political communities, I still felt incredibly judged. It was like an ultra-heightened experience of not being allowed in the cool-kid club in high school—but with all new rules that I had not learned and that no one took the time to explain to me. The language I grew up with could no longer be applied and would sometimes get me kicked out of social settings. My entire experience of growing up was judged and I felt totally isolated in trying to figure out why.

As I've gotten older, I've figured out the "right way" to navigate in these communities by learning language, protocol, and radical terminology while dropping the offensive and oppressive slang. I don't disagree with changing language to support systems we care about. I do disagree with judging people for not knowing the rules—especially since radicals are often organizing in favor of marginalized communities who are generally not aware of these rules.

If I wanted to fill out a form to describe my identity, I could check a bunch of boxes that would make my experience worth standing up for: Queer. Trans. Person of Color. Former Sex Trade Worker. Ironically, the biggest advocates for people like me—the people ready to throw down stats about harm reduction and youth, gender queer folks, and the vulnerable people in society—had no patience for me. I came into their communities looking for support, friends, and direction. I came having left abusive and sexually manipulative partners. I came in hella lost, unaware, and not very educated. But I came in agreement with their political perspectives because I knew society was fucked from the time I was twelve—maybe even younger. In high school, while other kids wrote about teen heartbreak, I wrote about injustices I saw everywhere. I came into these radical communities wanting to make change, but all my habits and the language I had learned to protect myself with got me in shit. When I was nineteen, I heard someone tell my older sister that they thought I spoke like I was "uneducated," and I lost it. Yes, I was uneducated, and they didn't recognize I had experienced things they would probably never understand.

People, including myself, can write as many articles, blog posts, and books as we want about what it means to be an ally, organizer, activist, or whatever we want to call ourselves. At the end of the day, what we are is human. And at our best, we are humble. We are learning. We have jumped off the high horses that colonialism so badly wants us to ride, and we are supportive of each other. We are unlearning our horrible and self-destructive habits, and we are

doing our best not to take it personally when others are not there with us (yet). We are recognizing the destructiveness of the systems that cause these habits rather than pointing fingers and blaming each other for having them, because we all do. Whether or not we have learned to unlearn derogatory sayings like "crazy," "gay," or "lame," we are learning to recognize the internal work we each are doing and do our best to support it. I am lucky to have a sister who—despite my anger issues and aggressive attitude—recognized I was working on myself, and she went out of her way to support me.

I want to be thankful to the women and lesbians who came before me for their fight because, straight up, I'll never know what it is to have so few rights, to not have a vote or be in public with my partner. I want to let go of the resentment I feel towards people who don't have the analysis, capacity, power, community, or education to unlearn specific internalized systems of oppression that I have learned to recognize in many privileges. I want to let go of the fact my first sponsor in AA disrupted my Step 5 to insert her political feminist perspectives, invalidating my experience as a queer trans person. I want to be aware that a lot of my survival has to do with the fact that I am able-bodied, thin, and hold conventionally attractive traits, granting me cute privilege—which is very important in our society and is something a lot of people don't spend enough time deconstructing. It means I can get decent jobs with fair bosses. I can meet people willing to hang out with me until five in the morning to tell me about the history of misogyny and women's rights. My privilege allowed me to be a stranger in a bilingual city and still be offered a full-time job on the spot (minimum wage, but still, I could pay my rent).

One of the things I am saddest about is how I've changed the way I relate to cisgender white people, and cis-men in general. I used to mostly hang out with cis-guys, all my life, and now I hang out with very few. I notice when I meet new cis-dudes, my chest tenses up and I start to put together the different oppressive patterns I've learned to recognize many cis-men perpetuate, like, for example, how white cis-dudes tend to take up space in conversations, meetings, at work, in art and music scenes, or how these men often refuse to acknowledge many difficult experiences they personally never have to feel as white men, but which are experienced daily by people living in the margins.

I know that we, humans of this colonial culture, are very susceptible to recognizing patterns and fitting things into boxes. I hope that these patterns and boxes start to change. Instead of primarily criticizing ways we are different, and not good enough, I hope we start changing our narratives to acknowledge and celebrate those differences, and to hear each other respectfully to be better in our differences. I see how deeply we criticize each other, and how that perpetuates segregation amongst our communities. The truth is, we really need to come together and connect experiences. Changing things for the better will take everyone. Including everyone takes mindful openness and listening to hold and make space for people of diverse communities.

While writing this, my younger bro has voiced he finds my language exclusive and judgmental. I sometimes try to point out how certain terms he uses—the same terms I have learned to stop using—perpetuate oppressive stories about people of marginalized groups. I found his statement super interesting and timely, and told him about this paper—like, "Hey, I'm writing about this exact thing! I get it. I don't want to act offended by your experience, or judge you, but also know I'm trying to get this message across to people in my community because I've felt their judgment, too." My brother, being the open-hearted person he is, heard my perspective and agreed that yes, it makes sense to change our language if we want to change the dominant narratives our language gives power to, but that people should also be sensitive to others' experiences and be open to meet them where they're at. To this, my older sister, being the great listener she is, summed it up and concluded that people who are using offensive language should also make an effort to unlearn terms that they can recognize are offensive, instead just avoiding saying "That's gay!" around their queer siblings. To which my brother responded, "Haha, word."

## ABOUT THE AUTHOR

*Kelsey Cham C. is a community organizer and settler of Chinese and Irish descent. Being involved with projects like the Purple Thistle in Vancouver, Canada has brought depth and insight into trying to understand what the hell is going on in the world. Kelsey is focused on organizing experiential learning projects with youth and adults in gardening, mycology, fermentation, and "ki" (chi) based karate.*

# LISTENING FOR A MULTIPLICITY OF QUIET RUMOURS WITHIN THE ANARCHA-FEMINIST ARCHIVE:

## A REVIEW OF *QUIET RUMORS: AN ANARCHA-FEMINIST READER*, NEW EDITION (AK PRESS, 2012)

- - - - - - - - - - - - - -

RAEANNA
GLEASON-SALGUERO

I n their 1971 manifesto, "Anarcha-Feminism: Two Statements," the Red Rose and Black Maria Black Rose Anarcho-Feminists define anarchism as "the affirmation of human freedom and dignity expressed in a negative, cautionary term signifying that no person should rule or dominate another person," and they encourage libertarian socialist feminists to cultivate "all the groovy things people can do and build together, once they are able to combine efforts and resources on the basis of common interest, rationality, and creativity" (15). In a radical response to the repressive, violent, and "pathological structure" of the State, they conclude this manifesto with a demand for "ALL POWER TO THE IMAGINATION!" (17). Anthologized within the Dark Star Collective's *Quiet Rumors: An Anarchist-Feminist Reader*, the Red Rose and Black Maria Black Rose manifesto opens the collection as a reminder of the need to be ever creative in our feminist approaches—also, to collectively imagine and manifest complex transformations in how people might relate to one another outside the crushing structures of power and hierarchical notions of human value.

*Quiet Rumors* provides anarcha-feminists and other readers with a solid archive of political inquiry stretching across two centuries and engaging the debates, disappointments, and dreams expressed within critical moments in multiple liberation movements. In its third edition, the 2012 publication of the collection aims to foster a sense of historical continuity and to share "a small portion of contemporary conversations and investigations of the anarchist movement" (7). However, while there is some useful archival material within the book, the structure of the text detracts from this material by only vaguely tracing historical linkages and neglecting to contextualize the important conversations. Incomprehensibly, the order and presentation of anthologized material lacks any discernible organizational structure or thematic categorization. The editors also fail to provide biographical or historical blurbs about the contributors or publication dates for their writing. These omissions are frustrating and render navigation of the material haphazard and decontextualized, which makes the text less accessible to those attempting to learn about anarcha-feminism with little or no background knowledge. Additionally, some of the historical texts speak through such generalizing terms that reading them evoked little interest, even as an archival resource. For example, essentialist and generalizing perspectives like Lynne Farrow's claims regarding how Black women's poetry perpetuates "self-deprecation" in order to "build Black men's egos" or that "women are suspicious of logic" are condescending, alienating, and weak. At a moment in which there are so many complex and necessary feminist discussions regarding internal racism and the reproduction of limiting notions of gender and sex, it is difficult to find value in tired texts like Farrow's. The role of the archivist is not to simply share *all* historical material

available, but rather to carefully select and curate key material that continues to speak to readers by offering stimulating historical legacy.

*Quiet Rumors* does include some provocative historical texts, however, that can inspire further thought. Emma Goldman's "A Woman Without a Country" and "The Tragedy of Woman's Emancipation" remain fresh for contemporary readers. The historical conditions Goldman discusses are continued to be experienced through the brutal violence produced by national boundaries and definitions of citizenship. We can connect to her when she says "Citizenship has become bankrupt," and a tool for targeting "undesirables," via practices of deportation, exile, and incarceration (98-99). Additionally, she questions a limited understanding of women's emancipation stilted by "artificial stiffness and its narrow respectabilities, which produce an emptiness in woman's soul" (103). She asserts that liberation cannot be achieved by "superficial equalization" efforts that provide surface level change but fail to initiate deeper transformation. Her discussion resonates with the often-cited debate included in *Quiet Rumors* between Jo Freeman's "The Tyranny of Structurelessness" and Cathy Levine's "The Tyranny of Tyranny." Both authors explore the extent to which structure and flexibility influence gendered burnout and movement exhaustion. Like Goldman, they strive to determine how people might best achieve liberation unfettered by invisible manifestations of power and authority. Freeman's position about elitism and how informal networks reproduce power relations in insidious forms holds great relevance. Women of color and queer people continue to issue nuanced critiques of similar silences and exclusions embedded within feminist and anarchist intellectual and activist spaces.

Unfortunately, while the preface of *Quiet Rumors* advocates the need to engage racial justice activism, to understand "the struggle for queer and trans rights," and to question "the logic of the gender binary," the collection feels mostly flat and uninspired in this task, missing a significant opportunity in this fairly recent third edition update. Stacy/Sally Darity's "Anarcha-Feminism and the Newer 'Woman Question'" and J. Rogue and Abbey Volcano's "Insurrection at the Intersections" are the most interesting as they complicate definitions of feminism and the grounds for collective mobilization. They consider gender oppression multidimensionally and intersectionally, denaturalizing the coherence of gender and sex categories and exposing them as unstable and constructed within dualistic and essentialist frameworks of conquest and coercion. While these essays open up important discussions, the collection fails to deeply capture the imagination, energy, and impact of queers and feminists of color both historically and currently. As queer and trans communities, poor people, and communities of color struggle to survive the profound violence of the prison industrial complex, militarized border policing, abusive medical systems, murderous police, labor exploitation, etc., this collection feels inadequate. The inclusion of the above essays as well as the interview with Mujeres Creando, though a bit dated, inch toward a more relevant discussion. In a time when the Black community powerfully demands that we bear witness and #sayhername,

this collection barely hints at the concrete lives asserting dignity and striving for liberation within the complex intersectionalities white feminists and anarchists have ignored and tokenized for far too long.

Returning to the Red Rose and Black Maria Black Rose manifesto, we are reminded of a need to be far more thoughtful in our archival and curatorial efforts, to consider access and relevance in more concrete and complex ways, to be imaginative and groovy rather than boring and stagnant. The invigorating appeal to all things groovy was a bright spot in the reading of this collection. Hinting at an affective relationship to rhythm, to the feeling that emerges in the groove of a record, the manifesto's desire for the groovy speaks to a need often lost as movements stagnate uncreatively in the obvious, or lazily fail to truly hear the full range of voices demanding liberation.

## ABOUT THE AUTHOR

*Raeanna Gleason-Salguero is a feminist professor at East Los Angeles College. She also serves as a coordinator for a community college Social Justice themed program advocating access to higher education and liberatory models of learning.*

letters from survivors of sexual violence

edited by lisa factora-borchers
introduction by aishah shahidah simmons

# FROM OBLIVION TO POLITICAL RESPONSIBILITY:

## AN ANARCHIST SISTER REVIEWS *DEAR SISTER: LETTERS FROM SURVIVORS OF SEXUAL VIOLENCE* (AK PRESS, 2014)

## SARA RAHNOMA-GALINDO

Radicals, including many anarchists, are involved in actively organizing against gender and sexual violence around the world. For example, Operation Anti-Sexual Harassment/Assault in Egypt; *Las Kallejeras* in the shantytowns of Santiago, Chile; the *Colectiva de Gafas Violetas* in Mexico; and countless other local initiatives all confront perpetrators in workplaces and organizing work. Yet, the task of addressing sexual violence, even in anarchist circles, continues to be singled out as primarily the job of survivors and their most immediate circles, instead of as a collective political responsibility. As an issue that we are socialized to meet with silence and stigmatization, sexual violence is commonly underemphasized or obscured amongst both radicals and society at large. Take for instance, ignorance of the fact that one out of three women in the world will be raped at some point in their lives. Or that, in the US, ninety-one percent of reported rape survivors are women, the most vulnerable being queer and gender nonconforming youth and people with physical disabilities, and fifteen percent of children are survivors of rape and incest. It is critical that our politics be aware of and address this. We need to be more diligent and active in both understanding sexual violence and linking it to radical organizing.

Consider reading *Dear Sister: Letters from Survivors of Sexual Violence* (AK Press, 2014), an anthology containing fifty insightful pieces, written by survivors from all walks of life, as part of this process. The book features an introduction by African-American incest and rape survivor and filmmaker Aishah Shahidah Simmons, and is edited by Philipina-American feminist author and survivor advocate Lisa Factora-Borchers. Known for having extensive involvement with survivors via coalition work, nonprofits, and institutions of higher education before piecing together *Dear Sister*, Lisa Factora-Borchers was first approached by Black feminist author Alexis Pauline Gumbs who asked her to write a letter of support to a friend who had just been raped. Not knowing the survivor's situation, her name, or much else about her, Lisa Factora-Borchers nevertheless acknowledge the situation and communicated support. Hence the idea for the book was born.

Lisa Factora-Borchers repeats this act of letter writing in *Dear Sister*, but this time with the assistance of a wealth of direct experiences from dozens of survivors, sharing experiences that have pushed their survival forward. Taken together, these brave narratives, and in particular those from women of color, queer, physically disabled, and working class perspectives, are valuable in and of themselves because they are not readily available elsewhere. I encourage readers to review the biographies at the back of the book to learn more about these amazing survivors.

The book is thematically organized and presented as a collection of traditionally-styled letters, poetry, essays and interviews with the editor. The first section is entitled "What Every Survivor Needs to Know," in which the authors remind readers of the importance of self-value while trying to understand the larger scheme of power disparities. Contributor 'An Ally' opens up with an affirmation, "yes...maybe the whole world is broken...but there is something that is not broken. You can find it" (29). Shanna

Katz speaks about survivor resilience and how "the power to re-enter the world as a strong(er), powerful woman" is the survivor herself (34). Renee Martin assures us that things will change for the best, because change is inevitable and survivors will "put this beside you and not behind you" (41). Lisa Factora-Borchers interviews Zoe Flowers, the author of *Dirty Laundry: Women of Color Speak Up About Dating and Domestic Violence*, who recalls the legacies of patriarchy and colonialism on survivors of color, reiterating that "we have been 'free' for a shorter period of time than we were oppressed" (48). Zoe Flowers's analysis highlights the ongoing impacts of colonialism and patriarchy, which perpetuate both objectification and violence against poor women of color.

"A Child Re-Members," is the name of the second section of the anthology. It takes on child rape and incest, gendered double-standards imposed on minors, and domestic violence against the entire household. Though sporadic and maybe too brief, authors give insight into the complexities of the nuclear family, gender norms instilled at birth, and the need to break out of them for everyone's survival. Juliet November shares that she always understood being a woman meant being prey to someone or something (73), and how heteronormativity designated the female body to a predisposition of abuse and violence (78). Contributor Sarah Cash explains being physically punished and labeled a bad girl, a flawed child, by a relative who "caught her being raped." Working through this experience, many years down the road, Cash learned to love herself as an outcast and in turn learned to love and struggle among society's flawed (61). Mary Zelinka consoles readers about not having a defined path forward, but shares her story encouraging all to always remember that, in one's journey of understanding, the violence incurred during our childhood is the fault of someone who chose to hurt us, and that it's not the survivor's fault (63). This section also includes a short essay by Kathleen Ahern that laments the death of her sister to commercial sexual exploitation as a child (70). [Their/her/his] mention of the early formation of coping mechanisms and the continuation of their repercussions into adulthood is a topic I wish had been formally introduced in the book, since it is randomly mentioned but not bundled for focused thinking.

The third section, "Family Ties," expands the described and reflected upon experiences to include the complexities of the nuclear family in relation to capital, immigration, and incarceration. The stories shared spill outside personal experience to include survivors' larger communities. Authors speak about class; about how poverty is the main reason battered moms and abused children had to stay at home with their perpetrator fathers despite abuse (81); and how survivors had to lie and intervene against social workers and police to avoid being put in foster care, or their family members being put in prison. Activist Mattilda Berstein Sycamore's essay reflects on the need to deconstruct masculinity so that the "brothers" don't fall into patriarchal cycles of violence. She recalls seeing "the way that masculinity created the walls I was trying to escape," and demands our accountability towards unlearning it (84). In a very thorough and beautifully written piece, organizer Amita Y. Swadhin bridges the connection between her survival of incest and that of other people the system had failed, in her case youth of color (101). She highlights how her organizing efforts helped channel rage into youth power and work that could fight "back against all the forms of injustice that had derailed my own youth" (105). If you take anything away from this anthology it should be this: many survivors have been effective in connecting their own stories of violence and survival to those of other disadvantaged sectors of society.

"From Trauma to Strength," the fourth section, gathers essays in support of self-definition and suggests paths for moving forward. While there is no uniform method, some pieces throughout the anthology mention the need for accountability and a few bring up transformative justice. As I understand it, transformative justice (TJ) propose respecting the survivor's agency. TJ also seeks accountability from those who harm, as well as community accountability and transformation of social conditions that perpetuate violence. Mia Mingus, a queer, physically disabled Korean organizer writes a superb essay to explain how the transformative justice framework "could hold the complexities of intimate and state violence, accountability, and healing and systemic and personal transformation" (140). Mingus explains that TJ is about addressing violence in ways that "don't cause more harm...don't collude with state (prison, police, the criminal legal system, etc.) or systemic (racism, sexism, etc.) violence... [and seek] individual and collective justice" for all those impacted. It would be naïve to think that survivors seek only individual justice, and Mingus speaks of healing as a far-reaching endeavor (145), similarly to what keysha willias and Leah Kashmi Piepza-Samarasinha say when speaking of this healing being counter-intuitive to the capitalist logic of destruction. They proclaim a halt to the self-destructive tendencies of our communities, as we are all interdependent (150).

In their eyes, the opposite of destructiveness would be constructing something else, perhaps not Transformative Justice necessarily, but what that is is yet to be defined.

The fifth section is titled "Radical Companionship," in which author Alexis Pauline Gumbs contributes an entertaining free verse piece titled "&," expressing supportive words amidst daily activities, intended not only during high points but also during low ones. Rebecca Wyllie de Echeverria shares the effects of incest and its physical aftershocks that inevitably manifest in survivors' long-term health. She encourages self-care and the shared [nature/condition] of struggle, emphasizing that "surviving is the process of finding new connections each day" (168).

The final section of *Dear Sister* is titled "Choose Your Own Adventure." It highlights many different activities and various directions survivors have gone in order to process and deal with the violence that did not kill them. The editor of the impactful book, *The Revolution Starts at Home*, Leah Lakshmi Piepzna-Samarasinha, gracefully shares her "Healing Mix Tape" music recommendations (188), while sci-fi author and co-editor of *Octavia's Brood* (IAS/AK Press, 2015), adrienne maree brown, encourages the overriding of shame or guilt to remember that "everything we do to survive is smart." (198) She cheerfully points out that counseling and sci-fi writing helped her a great deal. The final essay in this section is an interview the editor held with the Los Angeles poet Sofia Rose Smith. Together they point to the concepts of trauma with respect to the decision of whether or not to forgive perpetrators, referring back to Transformative Justice principle of humanizing those who have harmed us. In conjunction,

they discuss the binaries of survivor and perpetrator, along with the cultural norms of imposing the pace and modes of survivor healing. Whereas the beginning of the book apologizes to survivors and readers for showing no defined path to follow, the contributors focus not on one single way towards healing, restoration or reconciliation, but rather take for granted that they have gathered only a handful among myriad potential paths.

To understand sexual violence, it does not suffice to read about patriarchy, capitalism, or colonialism from a solely theoretical standpoint, even if you think you understand the complicated intersections that have rendered Black, brown, female, gender non-conforming, and queer bodies as disposable and subject to inevitable violence. Just as you would appreciate hearing workers' stories, testimonies about fighting police violence as a young brown person, or about neighbors resisting evictions, you should also be willing to hear survivor narratives like these. Some will say this is way too heavy of a topic for a such a little book, and that it can only be read in little bits at a time. I say the opposite: absorb it all, all at once. Read every single line to become well acquainted with the characteristics of this dominating apparatus. *Dear Sister* will place your survivor or supporter feet on firmer ground, as we work to build the necessary culture and counter-institutions to walk alongside all survivors.

## ABOUT THE AUTHOR

*Sara Rahnoma-Galindo is a survivor of sexual violence, anarchist person of color, office worker, student and board member of the Institute for Anarchist Studies, currently living in Los Angeles.*

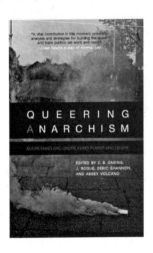

# FREE UNICORNS:

## A REVIEW OF *QUEER-ING ANARCHISM: ADDRESSING AND UNDRESSING POWER AND DESIRE*, EDITED BY C.B. DARING, J. ROGUE, DERIC SHANNON, ABBEY VOLCANO (AK PRESS, 2012)

- - - - - - - - - - - - - - -

## KRISTIAN WILLIAMS

*Queering Anarchism.* The title suggests a process, something in motion, developing, unfolding, undefined, unsettled. Indeterminacy is part of the point of the subversion of categories, an opening of possibilities, simultaneously emphasizing and easing difference. What was once hidden becomes apparent; what was once obvious becomes absurd. Both the anarchic and the queer challenge the status quo. Both expand our sense of the possible, enlarge our idea of freedom. What happens when these two mercurial concepts come into contact?

In making the attempt, *Queering Anarchism* accomplishes something remarkable, providing a good, quick orientation to anarchism and a short introduction to queer politics and queer theory. And by relating the two, it enacts a kind of intervention into each. The book's twenty-one chapters show that queer politics needs an analysis of class and power, and that the anarchist critique of capitalism and the state has much to gain by incorporating questions of gender and sexuality. The contributors consider the multiple ways that power relations shape our sex lives, our gender expressions, our family arrangements, our sense of self and belonging, and even our desires, fantasies, and entertainment. Conversely, they also explore the ways that freedom might change those things—and moreover, how changing them might in turn transform our understanding of freedom. As Jerimarie Liesegang writes in "Tyranny of the State and Trans Liberation":

> Whereas anarchists and anarchist theory need to look at struggle on the conceptual level that queer theory provides, queer theory needs to be coupled with anarchism's critique of structural domination, such as the state and capitalism. (96)

If that sounds a bit like a dare, it is a dare worth taking.

But dares do not always succeed. Many of the contributors indulge in some unwarranted leaps of logic, and more (perhaps most) suffer from an excess of optimism about their own intellectual and political projects¬ suggesting, for instance, as Liesegang does in that same essay, that queers are "truly inherently revolutionary peoples" (96). The result is an intellectual recklessness and occasional obsession with the first person singular, which sometimes manages to be charming but is equally likely to annoy. One of the longest essays in the book, provocatively titled "queering heterosexuality," amounts to little more than a strangely unrevealing all-lower-case rumination on the author's emotional growth. Another writer, likewise lacking any sense of self-effacing irony, settles into the view that "the most radical thing I do is meditate daily" (73). This is partly the result of looking through the wrong end of the "personal is political" telescope, but sometimes it is just a matter of getting carried away by an exciting idea, exaggerating its significance and swelling our expectations. Luckily, other contributors recognize the risks and, while pressing

a radical analysis as far as it can go, also skillfully flirt with the ridiculous as captured in the book's closing line: "And everybody gets a unicorn" (236).

In general, the prose in *Queering Anarchism* is pleasant and engaging, and remarkably free of the Foucault/Butler aesthetic of opacity. So readers will notice that the various authors do not always agree. Definitions of queer, approaches to anarchism, political strategies, philosophical traditions, and styles of argument all vary within the volume. That is, of course, all to the good. And those divergences, arguments, and contradictions only make more notable the themes that recur across multiple chapters. Among these are warnings against inverting (rather than dismantling) hierarchies, the view that "queer" is not an identity but a refusal of identities, and the insistence that no matter how you dress, or with whom you sleep, "queer liberation is for everyone" (226).

More than anything else, *Queering Anarchism* is a refreshing read. It is, on the whole, thoughtful but not obscure; challenging but never hectoring; and substantive as well as fabulous.

## ABOUT THE AUTHOR

*Kristian Williams is the author of* Our Enemies in Blue: Police and Power in America, *American Methods: Torture and the Logic of Domination,* Hurt: Notes on Torture in a Modern Democracy, *and* Fire the Cops! *He is a member of the Perspectives collective and the Institute for Anarchist Studies. He lives in Portland, Oregon.*

# BROODING OVER REVOLUTION AND BENDING REALITIES:

SCI-FI AS SOCIAL MOVEMENT. A REVIEW OF *OCTAVIA'S BROOD: SCIENCE FICTION STORIES FROM SOCIAL JUSTICE MOVEMENTS* (2015, AK PRESS/IAS) AND *SISTERS OF THE REVOLUTION* (2015, PM PRESS)

KIM SMITH

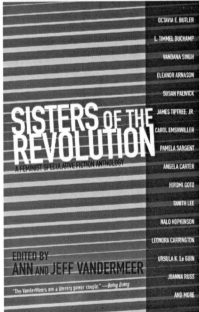

Too often I find myself giving into the urgency of organizing, of how this *struggle now* takes priority over pausing, imagining, reorganizing, reorienting, creating and recreating new worlds, new ways of relating. Of course organizers everywhere are also, everyday, creating many other worlds within this one, but too often it feels as though what takes center stage in our struggles are the analyses, critiques, and (of course) the too many, too long meetings that stand in for building something different. Spaces for risky, nonutilitarian creativity and inspiration are too often sidelined as inessential. Maybe the appearance of two sci-fi books (both from radical presses whose mainstays are political non-fiction) suggests that sci-fi is resurfacing as a relevant touchstone for contemporary political movements, signaling perhaps a bit more recognition of creative expression in explicitly political spaces. What exactly is the connection between sci-fi and radical movements and organizing? This question (and some ideas about how to answer it) emerged for me while reading these two humbling anthologies, which I'll get to in a moment, but first, a little more about these books.

While *Octavia's Brood* (2015, AK Press/IAS) and *Sisters of the Revolution* (2015, PM Press) appear initially as similar offerings from similar presses,

their differences are quite profound. While both are compilations of overtly politically-engaged sci-fi, the only near-overlap of content is that *Sisters of the Revolution* includes a brilliant story (one of the strongest in the collection) from the other book's namesake, Octavia Butler. Beyond this, they both specifically include writers "on the margins" of mainstream science fiction; in this way, many of the stories in each could be included in the other. The likening of one to the other is otherwise quite superficial, however, as the spirits that animate each anthology as a whole are clearly very different. *Sisters* is an historical compilation of pieces identified as "feminist speculative fiction" by its editors, Ann and Jeff VanderMeer, and seeks to bolster a feminist archive of science fiction, whereas *Brood* is "visionary fiction," highly cultural production emerging from and meant to feedback into contemporary social justice struggles. Taken each as collections, they each task science fiction with a different function in contemporary politics, and in doing so fill very different niches, and leave the reader with different orientations towards social change and how it happens.

*Sisters* is an anthology of previously-published, short feminist speculative fiction, including works as old as Anne Richter's 1967 "The Sleep of Plants," and as recent as Rose Lemberg's 2012 "Seven Losses of na Re." The collection is well-stocked with award-winning pieces and authors, mostly published in the last thirty-five years. In quite a different spirit, *Brood* is a collection—gathered and edited by adrienne maree brown and Walidah Imarisha—of "social-justice" oriented work, mostly specifically written for this book: a grassroots project that eventually made its way to the Institute for Anarchist Studies (IAS) and AK Press. With a few exceptions, the authors are first-time writers who brown and Imarisha requested contribute to the collection. That the book includes a short non-fiction piece by death-row prisoner Mumia Abu-Jamal and an essay by Tananarive Due on the theme of change in Butler's work helps ground the political commitments of this collection.

*Octavia's Brood* offers Octavia Butler as its namesake and "north star." The late Octavia Butler, who died in 2006, was a firebrand independent Black feminist science fiction writer. She, while incredibly prolific, was among few mainstream-recognized Black women writers in this genre until recently. As Due outlines in her contribution to this volume, Butler not only wrote to help usher new worlds into this one, but also actively sought to have this world be one in which there were more Black sci-fi writers, more specifically Black women sci-fi writers. This book project is testimony to this legacy and inheritance.

While it is clear that the editors revere Octavia Butler for her work, it is equally clear that she is not the sole progenitor of this book's inspiration. Imarisha convincingly insists in the Introduction, "all organizing is science fiction," (3) and most of the pieces in this book were written by organizers. Clearly there are talented, creative people behind these stories, but more centrally, the spirit expressed in this collection is one of social engagement and collective change.

So Butler is a progenitor for this book, but so is struggle. As Imarisha notes, "for those of us from communities with historic collective trauma, we must understand that each of us is already

science fiction walking around on two legs. Our ancestors dreamed us up and then bent reality to create us."(5) This book emerges as small yet rich evidence of Imarisha and brown's larger life projects of helping communities dream and bend realities themselves, together.

What stands out most prominently about the book, though, is that the worlds created in it are not dystopian dead-ends – or at least the characters won't let them be that. Between the falling of the eponymous "Black Angel" created by Imarisha in her own contribution and the impossible choices faced by characters in Kalamu Ya Salaam's "Manhunters" and Dani McCalin's "Homing Instinct," the heart of so many of these stories lies in the ways the characters struggle, and their choices to do so.

The stories in this book do not emerge as scathing critiques of contemporary society through tales of dystopian near-futures (though elements of that are certainly there) and they do not ask us to invest in a particular path towards utopia. Rather, the feeling I have after reading this compilation is that there are many ways to struggle, and it is perhaps in this that both meaningful lives and radical social change emerges. It avoids the traps that much politically-engaged science fiction falls into: diagnosing the ills of contemporary society to the degree that it becomes a trap without movement, with no way out. This trap, I think, is what the editors are creating an alternative to when they describe their project as not just science fiction but visionary fiction.

Certainly, this collection is not the most polished. The few excerpts from longer pieces are quite hard to follow, but—I must say—creatively and tantalizingly so: it is clear that they were not included to be comprehensive but instead be tastes of the larger works; regardless, they don't flow easily alongside the rest of the collection. Beyond this, some of these works could be honed a little: we are often welcomed into elaborate worlds with different social structures and cultural norms without enough context to make them quite work in such a short space; additionally, as is the risk in science fiction, some of these stories come off as didactic. These shortcomings don't take away from the strength of this work, which is not about perfect polish, but about ongoing processes and growth. It reminds me that these are written by people with stories bursting out of them, where there is never a final product, but always experiences, always processes, always another contribution to be made to create something different, something else, which in turn, will continue to change.

If *Octavia's Brood* is the contemporary expression of the struggle to create new worlds from this one, *Sisters of the Revolution* is an anthology that asks us to remember some of the contexts from which sci-fi, more broadly, has come.

This collection of already-published writing includes the tried and true Ursula K. Le Guin, James Tiptree, Jr., and Octavia Butler, but also creates space for the more contemporary and (as yet) less canonical Hiromi Goto, Nalo Hopkinson, and Vandana Singh. Under the broad umbrella of "feminist speculative fiction," this is a formidable and important archive of polished work, and is a solid introduction to some creative stories that engage the broad problem of gender and patriarchy.

A feminist archive, however, will never be uncontroversial. From the perspective of mainstream science fiction, this compilation highlights voices and perspectives at its margins: it includes feminist voices spanning over fifty years. This creates a bit of a challenge for the collection: feminist movements of all stripes have radically changed how gender and sexuality are conceptualized (and lived) over this period—and whose experiences are reflected in those movements—but these changes are not tracked in this collection. If speculative fiction always has something to say about the present moment, but the work was written forty years ago, how do we read it now? And how do we read a collection of works written at different historical moments, in relation to different feminisms?

If there is, indeed, a singular feminism that emerges in this book, it is one very much in response to white hetero-patriarchy. Many stories in *Sisters of the Revolution* reflect the bleakness of the potential future: the worst of this contemporary patriarchal society taken to an extreme. The stories that do this are sobering, angering, clarifying, and accurate in many ways. Critically, though, in creating bleak worlds with no way out, and without credible resistance, these stories often leave an aftertaste of despair that I personally read sci-fi to avoid. There are other feminisms in here, however, from Nalo Hopkinson's imaginatively and ambiguously resistant "The Glass Bottle Trick" to the enticingly geeky and happily-ever-after-esque "The Grammarian's Five Daughters" by Eleanor Arnason, to Nnedi Okorafor's inspiring "The Palm Tree Bandit," in which movement and change is possible, creative and fun.

More critically, the feminism in many of these stories is one that conflates body parts, gender, and sexuality, especially in relation to men, but also for women in many stories. The most play happens at the level of gender, with women subverting femininity (LeGuin's "Sur") or sometimes just surviving in patriarchal societies taken to the allegorical extreme (Pamela Sargent's all too prognostic 1984 "Fears"). Rather than drawing upon the diversity of experiences of gender in contemporary society, or using the wiggle room between binaries and norms as prying points for new ways of being in the world – and bringing on new ones - these stories too often fall back on essentialized notions of gender, and the ways out of dystopia are often about individual survival and womanhood. Given contemporary gender politics, this trajectory certainly makes this collection feel dated, and the archival anthology that it, well, is.

Seeing it as such an anthology allows for the older pieces to stand out for their historical significance in pushing the envelope of mainstream science fiction, and also for their lasting creativity and inspiration; Butler's stellar 1987 "The Evening, the Morning, and the Night," which plays with genetics and inherited traits in a somewhat deterministic yet allegorical way, is an excellent example of this. Additionally, the more recent pieces are clearly in this lineage: challenging what emerges as the mainstream in the book into a still different future for speculative fiction. Rachel Swirsky's magical "Detours on the Way to Nothing" and Vandana Singh's innovative "The Woman Who Thought She Was a Planet" are some of the most creative contributions to the volume. In this new trajectory of feminist speculative fiction that the VanderMeers trace here, it is important to note that a significant number of the collected authors are women of color.

Read next to each other, *Octavia's Brood* and *Sisters of the Revolution* make very different contributions. *Brood* builds momentum and inspiration for social justice movements that take the arts seriously—and vice versa—whereas *Sisters* contributes to a much needed archive of feminist struggles and visions, though many of these stories do feel narrow and dated in the age of Idle No More, Black Lives Matter, and radical queer and trans politics. It is also important to note the stark absence of Indigenous writers in both these compilations; it would have been nice to see the work of Zainab Amadahy, among others, highlighted here.

While reading these collections, what kept coming to mind is something that Indigenous folks, people of color, and disabled folks often remind others of us about with respect to mainstream (post-) apocalyptic fictions: some people have already lived and are currently living through the apocalypse, yet the worlds created in science fiction so often don't include Indigenous folks, people of color, people with disabilities. While again, *Sisters* is not absent women of color, their contributions do not feel central to the feminism that emerges; in *Brood* this type of critique feels nearly implicit at its core: in fact, the radically subversive and clever "Hollow" by Mia Mingus does this with creative ease that does not feel like critique at all, but instead a welcoming. *Brood* feels like a welcoming, an opening to experiment and create new worlds not out of critique or shame, but a desire to be a part of something more beautiful. What Imarisha notes in the Introduction to *Brood*, however, may help contextualize *Sisters* in this; she says, "changes will occur that we cannot even begin to imagine, and the next generation will be both utterly familiar and wholly alien to their parents."(3) These books are odd relatives, indeed, though certainly not of the parent-child relation. Perhaps they are so alien to each other in many ways, but both necessary for the different roles they play.

## ABOUT THE AUTHOR

*Kim Smith is a cat-bicycle-book-resonance-machine. Trembling aspens and magpies speak to her from Edmonton/Papaschase Cree land in Victoria/Lekwungen Territories where she is holed up attempting to finish a Master's degree.*

# THE INSTITUTE FOR ANARCHIST STUDIES AT TWENTY

## PAUL MESSERSMITH-GLAVIN

The IAS has received applications for writing grants throughout various waves of organizing over the last two decades. From Zapatista solidarity organizers in the nineties, to anti-capitalist globalization activists in the early '00s, Occupy folks over the last several years, and most recently from those working under the banner of Black Lives Matter. In 1996, the IAS was established to do just that. We have offered material support in the form of funds that allow people to take time off work or hire childcare so they can devote time to reflection and writing.

Sometime in 1995, my friend and comrade Chuck Morse asked me to join a new organization he was forming to support the development of anarchist theory. He was inspired by right-wing think tanks that funded the development and dissemination of their ideas, and thought the antiauthoritarian Left would benefit from something similar. What he envisioned, he explained, was a group that would raise money and award grants to people to devote time to thinking and writing, thereby assisting anarchism to live up to its full potential. He felt that contemporary anarchists needed financial help in the task of elaborating an anarchism that adequately responded to current conditions.

I immediately said "Yes" to Chuck, and became part of the group that founded the Institute for Anarchist Studies (IAS). The idea of developing structured, directly democratic organizations was important to us, and founding an institute made sense. Chuck incorporated the IAS as a 501(c) 3 non-profit organization and away we went. We raised money through contributions of anything from twenty dollars from movement organizers, to several thousands from well-off radicals, and began soliciting applications for writing grants. The next year we also began publishing our newsletter, *Perspectives on Anarchist Theory*, the name for which came from a brochure Chuck had seen at his bank, *Perspectives on Banking*.

When the IAS was founded, I was a member of the Love and Rage Revolutionary Anarchist Federation. Love and Rage was an organization involved in local struggles and national mobilizations, with chapters throughout the US and Canada, and one that published *Amor y Rabia* in Mexico. People started turning toward anarchism with the collapse of the Soviet Union, and it fully came into its own with the mobilizations of the Direct Action Network's affinity groups and a black bloc at the World Trade Organization protests in Seattle. The 1990s gave birth to a resurgence of anarchism, with it becoming a leading tendency on the Left. Throughout this time, the IAS sought to aid a rigorous development of its ideas.

In the summer of 2004, *Perspectives on Anarchist Theory* merged with a journal, also started by Chuck Morse, a radical review of books called *The New Formulation*. This established *Perspectives* as more than an IAS newsletter, becoming a substantial journal of its own. In 2009 a new crew took over *Perspectives* publication, with Josh MacPhee doing all cover art and design, creating the version you hold in your hands. In 2017 *Perspectives* will celebrate its own twentieth anniversary.

In 2010, the IAS started a book series with AK Press called Anarchist Interventions (AI). Since then, we have published six well received books, including a basic introduction to anarchism; a history of Movement for a New Society, which showed links between organizers in the 1970s and '80s; revolution against climate catastrophe, drawing from the likes of the Frankfurt School and Hannah Arendt; decolonizing anarchism, addressing South Asian antiauthoritarianism; undoing borders, decolonization, and anti-imperialism; and anarchists against the wall, by people doing solidarity work in Palestine. We have new AI books in the pike. Last year we began publishing books outside the AI series (though also with AK Press), starting with the best selling sci-fi collection of short stories, *Octavia's Brood: Science Fiction from Social Justice Movements*, and continuing with this year's *Angels with Dirty Faces: Three Stories of Crime, Prison, and Redemption*, by Walidah Imarisha. Early next year, we will publish Kevin Van Meter's *Guerrillas of Desire: Notes on Everyday Resistance and Organizing to Make a Revolution Possible*.

IAS members on the scene in New York City during the birth of the Occupy movement in 2011 found a need for a common radical language, and produced a series of Lexicon pamphlets, defining basic ideas, including white supremacy, anarchism, colonialism, gender, and power. We raised money to produce 33,000 copies of these pamphlets, which we distributed for free throughout the country. This type of work has continued with support for people organizing in response to the rebellion in Ferguson and elsewhere, and the subsequent movement against the police. One of our members lived in Ferguson for six months, getting to know folks whom she subsequently interviewed for a piece in *Perspectives*.

In its twenty years, the IAS has given out over one hundred writing grants to people from over a dozen countries. Awarding writing grants has been a largely satisfying process, as we've seen ideas turn into wonderful, widely read essays and books, offering insights from organizers and thinkers. We continuously post original essays through *Perspectives* on our website, and also maintain a speakers' bureau, allowing people to bring anarchist writers and organizers to their area to assist in local activist work or to help spread antiauthoritarian ideas.

When the IAS was founded, feminist, queer, and anti-racist anarchists were working to better develop their ideas and presence in the movement. Today we take these connections for granted, but at the time, this was controversial. This is the type of anarchism the IAS supports; one in which we work to dismantle all forms of hierarchy and domination, not just the state and capitalism, while engaging in the hard, daily organizing necessary to get us closer to a new society.

Over its twenty years, the IAS has sought to fund folks outside of universities in this task, aiding working-class people, people of color, women, and those outside the gender binary. We have preferred work by those striving to make sense of their organizing, or examining contemporary conditions, rather than histories of Krondstat or the Spanish Revolution, for instance. Our funding priorities are to assist work that will help advance the struggle for a free society in the here and now, rather than purely academic exercises.

Several years ago we decided to better channel the essays funded by our grants into *Perspectives* by encouraging shorter essays, to be completed in six months. We have also become much more involved in working with new authors to craft their writing through extensive editorial involvement. We encourage clarity in ideas, and writing in an accessible fashion. The result is the *Perspectives* collective has intense involvement with helping less experienced writers develop their work, and many incredible essays have subsequently appeared in *Perspectives*.

Anarchism has not yet reached its promise of fully developing theories to help us make sense of the world. We should continue to better implement practical, workable solutions and build lasting organizations. We still need to create motivating visions of alternative futures to counter the increasingly dystopian nature of our lives. And we need to be creative in expressing our ideas through various print, visual and audio media, and in face-to-face organizing.

The vast majority of the work done by members of the IAS is voluntary. We donate our labor. We do this in addition to our wage jobs, political organizing, raising children, and living our lives. We have one part-time, paid administrator to help us keep it all together, and to whom we are forever grateful. You can help make sure the IAS continues into the increasingly uncertain future. It takes the help and generosity of hundreds of people to make it possible for the IAS to give thousands of dollars in writing grants every year, publish *Perspectives* and our books, and do all our other our work.

Please take a minute to go to our website (www.anarchiststudies.org) and make a donation, or sign up to make monthly contributions. Together we can make a difference.

## ABOUT THE AUTHOR

*Paul has been a part of the IAS since its founding, is a member of the* Perspectives *collective, and belongs to the Hella 503 Collective in Portland, Oregon. He is writing a book on climate change and capitalism, with a view towards organizing to stop it.*

# 2016 IAS WRITING GRANTS

- - - - - - - - - - - -

We would like to congratulate four recipients of IAS writing grants for 2016. We chose these four out of sixty-two applications. They are: Henna Räsänen, writing *Weltuntergang: A Queer Post-Apocalyptic Graphic Novel*; Jeremy Louzao, writing "The Friendly Neighborhood Anarchist: Embracing the Groundwork that Makes Revolutions Possible;" Mona Luxion, writing "#Printemps2015: Lessons from Québec's Stunted Anarchist Anti-Austerity Mobilization;" and Toshio Meronek, writing "They Won't Quit: LAGAI Queer Insurrection." Congrats! Our next deadline to apply for a writing grant is January 15th, 2017. Go to our website (anarchiststudies.org) and click on Grants.

## HENNA RÄSÄNEN

Henna Räsänen is a queer femme Berlin-based political comic artist and illustrator and worked as an editor for two political comic anthologies: Sikala—*Comics on Factory Farming* and *On The Way To Peace*, targeting governmental structures of violence. Henna draws regular cartoons for the feminist magazine Tulva (Finland), as well as strip comics for Ubik Magazine (Finland) and is part of the Finnish Femicomix network. Henna hosts comic workshops on queer norms, and has self-published two issues of *A Hypothetical Love Triangle* comic zine.

*Henna's project is titled, WELTUNTERGANG: A Queer Post-Apocalyptic Graphic Novel*

WELTUNTERGANG narrates the end of the world, told from an anarchist and queer perspective, set in the surprisingly lively ruins of Berlin, Germany. It follows on a small group of queers, scavenging and surviving a few years after the collapse. The graphic novel focuses on issues affecting the queer community, while simultaneously speaking to a broader audience, creating a world in which queer protagonists are not singled out, while specific queer issues come to importance. Dealing with community building and consensus decision-making strategies as a part of survival, *Weltuntergang* comments on the actual, alarming political landscape of Northern Europe. Through the characters' intersectional portrayals of various genders, races, classes, body types, abilities, ages and backgrounds, the novel employs dark, prickly humor, and like dystopian sci-fi often does, uses fiction to comment on our world.

### JEREMY LOUZAO

Jeremy Louzao is a long-time anarchist organizer in the Seattle area, partaking in global justice affinity groups, collective community info-shops, anti-violence support groups, youth empowerment non-profits, Guatemalan ex-guerrilla communities, and most recently focusing on high school teaching and school reform work.

*Jeremy's project is called "The Friendly Neighborhood Anarchist: Embracing the Groundwork that Makes Revolutions Possible"*

Anarchism's "beautiful ideal" has remained woefully underdeveloped as a sustained, strategic orientation for mass-based social struggle on the ground. Anarchism so often remains a mild contributor, a sort of token sidekick to revolutionary movements--rarely getting a stage to strut its full strategic stuff. This project will argue that contemporary antiauthoritarian currents have tremendous potential to break from stale and rigid models of organizing and to actually build a winning mass politics, by embodying a uniquely humble, yet strategic anarchist disposition toward radical groundwork. It will explore in-depth 1) how radicals can personally embrace uniquely antiauthoritarian approaches to mass work—as listeners, accomplices, connectors, educators, and cheerleaders; and 2) how we can solidify that mass work into actual popular power through expressly non-cadre forms of mass organization.

### MONA LUXION

Mona Luxion is a white settler living in Montreal/Tio'tia:ke, where they are a PhD candidate, and organizes against militarism and capitalism in various forms. Born and raised in Chicago, Mona's introduction to movement politics came through anti-imperial and environmental justice struggles in the early 2000s. Today, they can often be found preserving food with their roommates, facilitating workshops, and working to reconcile struggles for necessary public services and infrastructure with anti-state, antiauthoritarian politics.

*Mona's project is called "#Printemps2015: Lessons from Québec's Stunted Anarchist Anti-austerity Mobilization"*

Looking at the efforts to spark a broad-based social movement in opposition to the austerity budgets (*politique déficit zéro*) by Québec's Liberal government in 2014, this essay will draw on interviews with movement organizers as well as seasoned activists who remained on the sidelines in order to understand the aims and aspirations of the mobilization and why, despite widespread opposition to austerity across Québec society, the campaign failed to mobilize sustained large-scale participation. "#Printemps2015" will investigate the impact of the specter of Québec's massive student-led popular uprising in 2012 on organizing in 2014-2015, and the use of rhetoric highlighting the effects of austerity budgets on a wide variety of issues. The lessons of #printemps2015 are likely to be useful for other movement-building efforts, offering both a source of inspiration and a critique of the ways in which solidarity and intersectionality are practiced in North American anarchist organizing communities that are predominantly young, white, and university-adjacent.

## TOSHIO MERONEK

Toshio Meronek is an independent journalist focusing on politics, the Bay Area, disability, LGBT/queer issues, and prisons. He covers Silicon Valley for *TruthOut*, and has also reported for *Al Jazeera*, *In These Times*, and *The Nation*. His work has appeared in several anthologies—most recently in *Captive Genders: Trans Embodiment and the Prison Industrial Complex* (AK Press, 2015)

*Toshio's project is tentatively titled, "They Won't Quit: LAGAI Queer Insurrection"*

Plenty of flash-in-the-pan radical organizations have emerged for short periods only to dissolve quickly into the ether. Many have laid groundwork for future antiauthoritarian justice activism, but few have had the staying power of the San Francisco Bay Area's LAGAI—Queer Insurrection. Taking on often-unpopular but critical political positions, its comrades have popularized direct actions around the boycott, divestment and sanctions movement for Palestinian liberation; shut down the Golden Gate bridge to spotlight the AIDS crisis; and produced the longest-running prisoner-focused newspaper in the US, *UltraViolet*. Today's activists have much to learn from LAGAI's members, which include both lovers and frenemies, and people all over the gender spectrum. This project will attempt to figure out what extraordinary factors have led the group to thrive and stay true to its radical roots over multiple generations.

"A brave, honest search for answers regarding incarceration."
**—Kirkus Reviews**

NEW FROM AK PRESS & THE INSTITUTE FOR ANARCHIST STUDIES

# ANGELS WITH DIRTY FACES

THREE STORIES OF CRIME, PRISON, AND REDEMPTION

WALIDAH IMARISHA

AVAILABLE NOW AT AKPRESS.ORG
OR WHEREVER YOU BUY BOOKS.

# PLAY:

-------------

## A CALL FOR SUBMISSIONS FOR THE NEXT ISSUE OF *PERSPECTIVES*

Are you an organizer or activist currently engaged in movement work? Are you interested in taking time to reflect on the lessons and ideals of this work in order to help advance anarchist praxis? Are you a self-taught thinker with a particular interest or expertise in some aspect of radical history or practice? Are you willing to share your insights to contribute to our collective memory? Do you have ideas, experiences, or questions that you would like to develop and share with a wider audience?

If you answered "yes" to any of these questions, the *Perspectives on Anarchist Theory* editorial collective would like to hear from you. We believe it is crucial that those of us with visions of a free society share our work and ideas so that we can create a solid, common foundation on which to build a better world. We value underrepresented voices, accessibility, complexity, and the rigorous investigation of ideas.

We are currently accepting work related to the concept of "play," and encourage writers to conceive of the theme as broadly as possible. For some, "play" may conjure notions of mischief or the anarchic spirit. For others, it may provoke questions around creative street tactics and interventions, or the various roles of theater and performance in movement work. Pastimes, game theory, sports and sport culture, playfulness at all ages—all are fair game. We encourage folks to submit work that explores the transformative power of joy, challenge, and strategy.

We do not have a maximum or minimum word count, though shorter pieces do allow us to include more work by a broader range of authors. When submitting, please ensure first that you are familiar with the kinds of writing and scholarship *Perspectives* publishes, and that your document format adheres to the Chicago Manual of Style. All notes must be done as endnotes, not footnotes, and the note numbers must be typed directly into the body of the text. Authors are welcome to query in advance of submitting manuscripts. Editorial support is available to develop your idea or piece; first-time authors are encouraged to submit.

To submit or query, please email: PerspectivesonAnarchistTheory@ gmail.com. Submission deadline for the Play issue is **January 1, 2017.**